ALLEN LANE

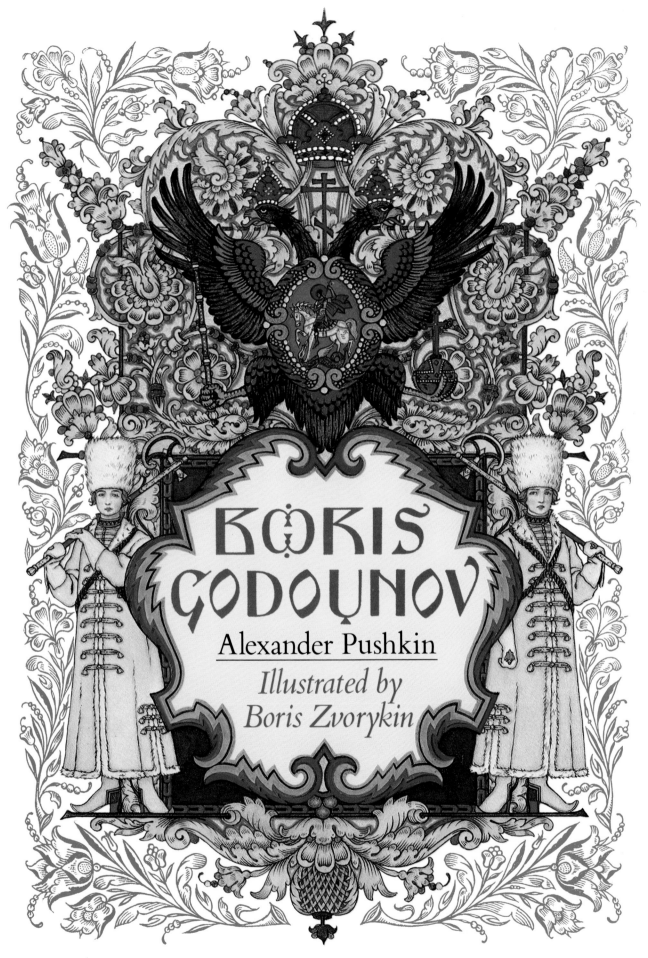

# BORIS GODOUNOV

## Alexander Pushkin

### Illustrated by
### Boris Zvorykin

Introduction by Peter Ustinov

ALLEN LANE
Penguin Books Ltd.
536 King's Road
London SW10 OUH

First published in the United States of America
by The Viking Press (A Studio Book) 1982
Published by Allen Lane 1982

ISBN 0 7139 1541 2

Grateful acknowledgment is made to
Routledge & Kegan Paul Ltd, London,
for permission to reprint Alfred Hayes's translation
of *Boris Godounov* from *The Poems, Prose
and Plays of Alexander Pushkin*.

The original edition from which the artwork
for this volume was reproduced was acquired
from the Rapolti Family Collection.

Printed in Japan
Set in Palatino

## List of Illustrations

# Introduction

In her introduction to the companion volume, *The Firebird and Other Russian Fairy Tales*, Jacqueline Onassis mentions a few salient facts about the life and career of Boris Zvorykin. Born in Moscow in 1872, he devoted himself to decorative art after graduating from the Moscow Academy of Painting. Although he painted the murals for the Cathedral at Simferopol and designed the patriarchal seal for the church, his fame stems mainly from his book illustrations.

It is fashionable, if inaccurate, to maintain that a rift in the development of Russian art occurred at the moment of the Revolution and that a great tradition was lost overnight in the upheaval, or at least that it petered out painfully in exile. In point of fact, although the October Revolution changed the social structure of the nation, the arts, crafts, and habits of the Russian people show the same dogged continuity through thick and thin, through light and darkness. After the terrible destruction caused by the Second World War, it is curious to note that peoples palpably addicted to traditions of royalty, like the British and the Dutch, were far less sentimental in their reconstruction than the Russians and the Poles, who painstakingly rebuilt palaces and other symbols of imperialism as part of an irreplaceable national heritage. Conversely, the kingdoms gave free rein to modern architects: a brand-new cathedral stands where a bombed-out shell once stood, like a broken tooth in the heart of Coventry. Had the calamity occurred in Russia, the Russians would have rebuilt what had been there before, using every trick of the trade to give the replica the patina of age and the serenity of time.

In short, the Russians are not only meticulous in all things artistic, but they are among the most instinctively conservative of all peoples. It takes an imperative, like the practical application of Marxist theory or the invasion of the mother country, to shake them momentarily out of the comfort of routine, but they quickly slide back into their ancient activities when the eyes of the authorities have been temporarily eluded or the bayonets of the enemy successfully laid low.

In recent history, Russia has been depicted either as a sleeping giant or as an insensitive bear rampaging over a landscape not its own. Neither image is any more representative than is the spare, angular figure of Uncle Sam or the obese and bulbous John Bull. It is conveniently forgotten (or was it ever known?) that Russia was once a small and anxious association of tribes, buffeted by the Mongol invasion, and held in subtle servitude by the smiling khans of the Golden Horde. This thralldom is practically without parallel in history, so long did it last and so insidious were its effects.

It is during times of hardship that a people creates its heroes, its John Paul Joneses and William Tells. The Russians are no exceptions. The princes Alexander Nevsky and Dimitri Donskoi are among the real yet legendary figures who inspired the earliest ballads—the former defeating the Teutonic knights and other invaders from the West while swallowing his pride by continuing to pay the ruinous tribute to the Tartars, the latter winning a famous victory over the Tartars on the field of Kulikovo, which diminished the financial obligation though it failed to eradicate it altogether.

The Tartar horde eventually drifted into decadence, while the Russians, with that typical mixture of patience and sense of community which has exasperated the countless invaders of their soil throughout history, managed to conserve their strength and even to increase it by the first great cohesive surge—a consciousness of nationhood—which was marked by the victory of Moscow over the other principalities and the commercial republic of Novgorod.

The epoch of Boris Godounov marked a pause in the all too rapid development of the nation. It was a period of indigestion, of absorption, and of chaos. Boris belonged to the minor nobility, but by virtue of his high intelligence and political shrewdness he enjoyed the confidence of Ivan IV, known as "the Terrible." When Ivan was succeeded by his dimwitted son Feodor, Boris became the de facto ruler of this endlessly emerging nation, conducting successful campaigns against the greedy intrusions of Swedes, Poles, and Crimean Tartars. In 1598, with the death of Feodor, Boris was elected czar by the Zemsky Sobor, a kind of Privy Council of nobles, merchants, and clerics. Despite his promises of a rosier future, the disastrous redistributions of land undertaken by his predecessors to strengthen the central government at the expense of the landed gentry eventually resulted in administrative upheavals and the degradation of the peasants, as well as the servitude of all and sundry to a monolithic autocracy. The consequences of this epidemic of confusion were uprisings, resistance, espionage, primitive confiscations of property, and, of course, famine. There were limitations on travel, and, worse still, conspiracies were formed, leading to deportations and death. A mysterious pretender appeared, claiming to be the youngest son of Ivan IV, Dimitry, who had died as a child. This strange precursor of Anastasia was the final fantasy in the long nightmare of Boris's reign, and it was not until the election of the first Romanov czar in 1613 that a degree of normalcy returned to the affairs of state and a new continuity, which was to last until 1917, could be set in motion.

It is these somber times which inspired Pushkin to write, Moussorgsky to compose, and Zvorykin to paint. If Moussorgsky was to invest Pushkin's epic poem with all the controlled waywardness of his genius—rough edges and splinters of sound perceptible in the choral majesty, shafts of character, and stabs of blinding light in the prevailing gloom, all forever disturbing, even shocking—Zvorykin veered toward the frozen stillness of the icons, capturing moments of the narrative and petrifying them with his arctic detachment. There is a feeling of utter immobility about his vision, and for all its pervading Victorianism, it has the conviction of authenticity, as though these fragments belong to some long-lost archive.

Pushkin, the reckless romantic, so carelessly killed in a stupid duel; Moussorgsky, the professional amateur, without staying power but with moments of sublime imagination; Zvorykin, the thorough, unquestioning academic, finding a way to be personal despite obedience to the exigencies of tradition; Boris Godounov, clever, ambitious, a gambler with the barely latent flaw, a conscience open to superstition and horrid yearnings for redemption—each in his way is a faithful reflection of Russianness.

With the oversimplifications of the contemporary political and ethical conflict, there is, alas, little time for such contemplations. Suffice it to say that no other nation in the world has lost so few of its sons on foreign soil compared with the enormous number of both sons and daughters it has lost on its own soil. It is a miracle that Russia survived its own early history, and the arts of Pushkin, Moussorgsky, and Zvorykin are, each in their own way and on their own level, faithful reflections of this miracle.

Peter Ustinov

БЖІЕЙ МИЛОСТІЮ
ВЕЛИКІЙ ГОСУДАРЬ
ЦРЬ И ВЕЛКІЙ КНЗЬ
БОРИСЪ ѲЕОДРОВИЧЪ
ВСЕА РУССІИ САМО
ДЕРЖЦЪ

# DRAMATIS PERSONAE

BORIS GODOUNOV, elective Czar
FEODOR, his son, the Czarevitch
XENIA, his daughter, the Czarevna
PRINCE SHUISKY
PRINCE VOROTYNSKY
SHCHELKALOV, Secretary of the Council of Boyars
THE PATRIARCH
FATHER PIMEN, monk and chronicler
AFANASY PUSHKIN, a nobleman
SEMYON GODOUNOV
BASMANOV, Commander of Godounov's army
MARGERET ⎱ foreign captains in Godounov's service
WALTER ROSEN ⎰
ROZHNOV, a prisoner of the Pretender
MISAIL ⎱ wandering monks
VARLAAM ⎰
GRIGORY OTREPYEV, a monk, afterwards Dimitry the
    Pretender
GAVRILA PUSHKIN ⎫
PRINCE KURBSKY ⎬ Russian supporters of the Pretender
KHRUSHCHOV ⎭
KARELA, a Cossack
SOBANSKI, a Polish gentleman
FATHER CZERNIKOWSKI, a Jesuit
WISNIOWIECKI ⎱ Polish magnates
MNISZECH ⎰
MARYNA, daughter of the latter
RUZIA, Maryna's maid
MOSALSKY ⎫
GOLITSYN ⎬ Boyars
MOLCHANOV ⎪
SHEREFEDINOV ⎭

The People, Boyars, a Wicked Monk, Abbot of the
Chudov Monastery, two Courtiers, Hostess, two Of-
ficers, Guests, Boy at Shuisky's, the Czarevna's
Nurse, a Poet, a Cavalier, a Lady, Serving-women,
Russian, Polish, and German troops, a Saintly Idiot,
Boys, Old Woman, the Pretender's Supporters,
Court Attendants, a Peasant, a Beggar, a Guard,
three Soldiers.

PALACE OF THE KREMLIN

(*20 February 1598*)

PRINCES SHUISKY *and* VOROTYNSKY

VOROTYNSKY. To keep the city's peace, that is the task
  Entrusted to us twain, but we forsooth
  Have little need to watch; Moscow is empty;
  For to the Monastery all have flocked
  After the Patriarch. What thinkest thou?
  How will this trouble end?

SHUISKY.                          How will it end?
    That is not hard to tell. A little more
    The multitude will groan and wail, Boris
    Pucker awhile his forehead, like a toper
    Eyeing a glass of wine, and in the end
    Will humbly of his graciousness consent
    To take the crown; and then—and then will rule us
    Just as before.

VOROTYNSKY.    And yet a month has passed
    Since, cloistered with his sister, he forsook
    the world's affairs. None hitherto hath shaken
    His purpose, not the Patriarch, and not
    His boyar counselors; their tears, their prayers
    He heeds not. Deaf is he to Moscow's wail,
    To the Great Council deaf; vainly they urged
    The sorrowful nun-queen to consecrate
    Boris to sovereignty; firm was his sister,
    Inexorable as he; methinks Boris
    Inspired her with this spirit. What if our Ruler
    Be sick in very deed of cares of state
    And hath no strength to mount the throne?
    What say'st thou?

SHUISKY. I say that then the blood of the Czarevitch
    Was shed in vain, that the poor child Dimitry
    Might just as well be living.

VOROTYNSKY.                    Fearful crime!
    Is it beyond all doubt Boris contrived
    The young boy's murder?

SHUISKY.                        Who besides? Who else
    Bribed Chepchugov in vain? Who sent in secret
    The brothers Bityagovsky and Kachalov?
    Myself was sent to Uglich, there to probe
    This matter on the spot; fresh traces there
    I found; the town bore witness to the crime;
    With one accord the burghers all affirmed it;
    And with a single word, when I returned,
    I could have proved the secret villain's guilt.

VOROTYNSKY. Why didst thou then not crush him?

SHUISKY.                                At the time
    I do confess, his unexpected calmness,

16

His shamelessness, dismayed me. Candidly
He looked me in the eyes; he questioned me
Closely, and I repeated to his face
The foolish tale himself had whispered to me.

VOROTYNSKY. An ugly business, prince.

SHUISKY.                                        What could I do?
  Declare all to Feodor? But the Czar
  Saw all things with the eyes of Godounov,
  Heard all things with the ears of Godounov;
  Grant even that I might have fully proved it,
  Boris would have denied it there and then,
  And I should have been haled away to prison,
  And in good time—like mine own uncle—strangled
  Within the silence of some deaf-walled dungeon.
  I boast not when I say that, given occasion,
  No penalty affrights me. I am no coward,
  But also am no fool, and do not choose
  Of my free will to walk into a halter.

VOROTYNSKY. Monstrous misdeed! Listen; I warrant you
  Remorse already gnaws the murderer;
  Be sure the blood of that same innocent child
  Will hinder his ascension to the throne.

SHUISKY. He'll not be balked; Boris is not so timid!
  What honor for ourselves, ay, for all Russia!
  A slave of yesterday, a Tartar, son
  By marriage of Maluta, of a hangman,
  Himself in soul a hangman, he to don
  The crown and cape of Monomakh!

VOROTYNSKY.                              You are right;
  He is of lowly birth; we twain can boast
  A nobler lineage.

SHUISKY.                    Indeed 'tis so!

VOROTYNSKY. Let us remember, Shuisky, Vorotynsky
  Are, let me say, born princes.

SHUISKY.                          Born princes, truly.
  And of the blood of Rurik.

VOROTYNSKY.                    Listen, prince;

17

Then we, 'twould seem, should have the right to
Mount Feodor's throne.

SHUISKY.                    Rather than Godounov.

VOROTYNSKY. In very truth 'twould seem so.

SHUISKY.                                    And what then?
    If still Boris pursue his crafty ways,
    Let us contrive by skillful means to rouse
    The people. Let them turn from Godounov;
    Princes they have in plenty of their own;
    Let them from out their number choose a czar.

VOROTYNSKY. We heirs of the Varangians are many,
    But 'tis no easy thing for us to vie
    With Godounov; the people are not wont
    To recognize in us an ancient branch
    Of their old warlike masters; long already
    Have we our appanages forfeited,
    Long served but as lieutenants of the czars,
    And he hath known, by fear, and love, and glory,
    How to bewitch the people.

SHUISKY. (*Looking through a window.*) He has dared,
    That's all—while we— Enough of this. Thou seest
    Dispersedly the people are returning.
    We'll go forthwith and learn what is resolved.


# THE RED SQUARE


### THE PEOPLE


FIRST MAN. He is inexorable! He thrust from him
    Prelates, boyars, and Patriarch; in vain
    They prostrated themselves before Boris;
    The splendor of the throne but frightens him.

SECOND MAN. O God, who is it will rule over us?
    Oh, woe to us!

18

THIRD MAN.          See! The Chief Minister
    Is coming out to tell us what the Council
    Has now resolved.

THE PEOPLE.          Silence! Silence! He speaks,
    The Minister of State. Hush, hush! Give ear!

SHCHELKALOV. (*From the Red Porch.*)
    The Council have resolved for the last time
    To put to proof the power of supplication
    Upon our Ruler's mournful soul. At dawn,
    After a solemn service in the Kremlin,
    The holy Patriarch will go, preceded
    By sacred banners, with the holy ikons
    Of Don and of Vladimir; with him go
    The Council, courtiers, delegates, boyars,
    And all the pious folk of Moscow; all
    Will go once more to pray the queen to pity
    Our orphaned Moscow, and to consecrate
    Boris unto the crown. Now to your homes
    Go ye in peace: pray; and to Heaven shall rise
    The heart's petition of the orthodox.
                    (*The* CROWD *disperses.*)


# THE MAIDEN FIELD

FIRST MAN. To plead with the Czarina in her cell
    Now are they gone. Thither have gone Boris,
    the Patriarch, and the boyars.

SECOND MAN.                    What news?

THIRD MAN. Still is he obdurate; yet there is hope.

PEASANT WOMAN. (*With a child.*)
    Drat you! stop crying, or else the bogie-man
    Will carry you off. Drat you, drat you! stop crying!

FIRST MAN. Can't we slip through behind the fence?

SECOND MAN.                    No chance!
    No chance at all! Not only is the nunnery

Crowded; the precincts too are crammed with
People. Look, what a sight! All Moscow has thronged
Here. See! fences, roofs, and every single story
Of the Cathedral bell tower, the church-domes,
The crosses too are studded thick with people.

FIRST MAN. A goodly sight indeed!

ANOTHER MAN.                              What is that noise?

SECOND MAN. Listen! What noise is that?—
   The people groan;
   See there! They fall like waves, row upon row—
   Again—again— Now, brother, 'tis our turn;
   Be quick, down on your knees!

THE PEOPLE. (*On their knees, groaning and wailing.*)
                                        Have pity on us,
   Our father! Oh, rule over us! Oh, be
   Father to us, and Czar!

FIRST MAN. (*Sotto voce.*) Why are they wailing?

SECOND MAN. How can we know? It's the boyars' áffair.
   We are small folk.

PEASANT WOMAN. (*With child.*)
                        Now, what is this? Just when
   It ought to cry, the child is still. I'll show you!
   Here comes the bogie-man! Cry, naughty child!
      (*Throws it on the ground; the child screams.*)
   That's right, that's right!

FIRST MAN.                    As everyone is crying,
   Come, brother, let us also start to cry.

ANOTHER MAN. Brother, I try my best, but can't.

FIRST MAN.                                        Nor I.
   Haven't you got an onion? Let us rub
   Our eyes with that.

SECOND MAN.            No; but I'll take some spittle
   To wet my eyes. What's up there now?

FIRST MAN.                              Who knows?

21

THE PEOPLE. The crown is his! He is the rightful Czar!
Boris consents at last! Long live Boris!


# THE KREMLIN PALACE

BORIS, PATRIARCH, BOYARS


BORIS. Thou, Father Patriarch, all ye boyars!
My soul lies bare before you; ye have seen
With what humility and fear I took
This mighty power upon me. Ah! how heavy
The weight of obligation! I succeed
The great Ivans; succeed the angel Czar!
Oh, righteous one, oh, sovereign father, look
From Heaven upon the tears of thy true servants,
Bestow on him whom thou hast loved, whom thou
Hast raised so high on earth, bestow on him
Thy holy blessing. May I rule my people
In glory, and like thee be good and righteous!
To you, boyars, I look for help. Serve me
As ye served him, that time I shared your labors,
Ere I was chosen by the people's will.

BOYARS. We will not from our plighted oath depart.

BORIS. Now let us go to kneel before the tombs
Of Russia's great departed rulers. Then
Bid all our people to a mighty feast,
All, from the nobleman to the blind beggar.
To all free entrance, all most welcome guests.
                                        (*Exit, the* BOYARS *following.*)

VOROTYNSKY. (*Stopping* SHUISKY.)
Thy guess was right.

SHUISKY.                    What guess?

VOROTYNSKY.                         Why, thou recallest—
The other day, here on this very spot.

SHUISKY. No, I remember nothing.

22

VOROTYNSKY.                             When the people
    Flocked to the Maiden Field, thou said'st—

SHUISKY.                                   'Tis not
    The time for recollection. There are times
    When I should counsel thee not to remember,
    But even to forget. And for the rest,
    I sought but by feigned calumny to prove thee,
    The better to discern thy secret thoughts.
    But see! the people hail the Czar—my absence
    May be remarked. I'll join them.

VOROTYNSKY.                          Wily courtier!

## NIGHT. CELL IN THE CHUDOV MONASTERY

*(The year 1603)*

FATHER PIMEN, GRIGORY *(sleeping)*

PIMEN *(Writing by lamplight.)*
    One more, the final record, and my annals
    Are ended, and fulfilled the duty laid
    By God on me, a sinner. Not in vain
    Hath God appointed me for many years
    A witness, teaching me the art of letters;
    A day will come when some laborious monk

Will bring to light my zealous, nameless toil,
Kindle, as I, his lamp, and from the parchment
Shaking the dust of ages will transcribe
My chronicles, that thus posterity
The bygone fortunes of the orthodox
Of their own land may learn, will mention make
Of their great czars, their labors, glory, goodness—
And humbly for their sins, their evil deeds,
Implore the Savior's mercy— In old age
I live anew; the past unrolls before me—
Did it in years long vanished sweep along,
Full of events, and troubled like the deep?
Now it is hushed and tranquil. Few the faces
Which memory hath saved for me, and few
The words which have come down to me—the rest
Have perished, never to return— But day
Draws near, the lamp burns low, one record more,
The last. (*He writes.*)

GRIGORY. (*Waking.*) The selfsame dream! Is't possible?
For the third time! Accursed dream! And ever
Before the lamp sits the old man and writes—
And not all night, 'twould seem, from drowsiness
Hath closed his eyes. I love the peaceful sight,
When, his calm soul deep in the past immersed,
He pens his chronicle. Oft have I longed
To guess what 'tis he writes of. Is't perchance
The dark dominion of the Tartars? Is it
Ivan's grim death-dealing, the stormy Council
Of Novgorod? Is it about the glory
Of our great fatherland? I ask in vain!
Not on his lofty brow, nor in his looks
May one perceive his secret thoughts; his aspect
Is still the same: lowly at once, and lofty—
Like to some Magistrate grown gray in office,
Calmly he contemplates alike the just
And unjust, with indifference he notes
Evil and good, and knows not wrath nor pity.

PIMEN. Art thou awake?

GRIGORY.                    Pray, honored father, give me
Thy blessing.

PIMEN.          May God bless thee on this day,
Yes, and forever after.

28

GRIGORY.                  All night long
  Thou hast been writing and abstained from sleep,
  While demon visions have disturbed my peace,
  The fiend molested me. I dreamed I scaled
  By winding stairs a turret, from whose height
  Moscow appeared an anthill, where the people
  Seethed in the squares below and pointed at me
  With laughter. Shame and terror came upon me—
  And falling headlong, I awoke. Three times
  I dreamed the selfsame dream. Is it not strange?

PIMEN. 'Tis the young blood at play; humble thyself
  By prayer and fasting, and thenceforth thy dreams
  Will all be bright and airy. Even now,
  If I, grown weak for want of sleep, should fail
  To make my orisons of wonted length,
  My senile sleep is neither calm nor sinless;
  My dreams hold riotous feasts, or camps of war,
  And skirmishes, the wild, insane diversions
  Of youthful years.

GRIGORY.            How joyfully didst thou
  Live out thy youth! The fortress of Kazan
  Thou fought'st beneath, with Shuisky didst repulse
  The Lithuanian host. Thou'st seen the court,
  And splendor of Ivan. Ah! happy thou!
  Whilst I, from boyhood up, a wretched monk,
  Was it not given to play the game of war,
  To revel at the table of a czar?
  Then, like to thee, would I in my old age
  Have gladly from the noisy world withdrawn,
  To vow myself a dedicated monk,
  And in the quiet cloister end my days.

PIMEN. Complain not, brother, that the sinful world
  Thou early didst forsake, that few temptations
  The All-High sent to thee. Believe my words;
  The glory of the world, its luxury,
  Woman's seductive love, seen from afar,
  Enslave our souls. Long have I lived, have taken
  Delight in many things, but never knew
  True bliss until that season when the Lord
  Guided me to the cloister. Think, my son,
  On the great czars; who loftier than they?

God only. Who dares thwart them? None. And yet
Often the golden crown became to them
A burden; for a cowl they bartered it.
The Czar Ivan sought in monastic toil
Tranquillity; his palace, filled erewhile
With haughty minions; grew to all appearance
A monastery; the very cut-throats whom
He chose for guardsmen became cowled monks
In shirts of hair; the terrible Czar appeared
A pious abbot. Here, in this very cell
(At that time Cyril, the much suffering,
A righteous man, dwelt in it; even me
God then made comprehend the nothingness
Of worldly vanities), here I beheld,
Weary of angry thoughts and executions,
The Czar; among us, meditative, quiet,
Here sat the Terrible; we motionless
Stood in his presence, while he talked with us
In tranquil tones. Thus spake he to the abbot
And to us all: "My fathers, soon will come
The longed-for day; here shall I stand before you,
Hungering for salvation; Nicodemus,
Thou Sergius, and Cyril, will accept
My holy vow; to you I soon shall come
A man accursed, here the clean habit take,
Prostrate, most holy father, at thy feet."
So spake the sovereign lord, and from his lips
The words flowed sweetly. Then he wept; and we
With tears prayed God to send his love and peace
Upon his suffering and stormy soul.
What of his son Feodor? On the throne
He sighed for the mute hermit's peaceful life.
The royal chambers to a cell of prayer
He turned, wherein the heavy cares of state
Vexed not his holy soul. God grew to love
The Czar's humility; in his good days
Russia was blest with glory undisturbed,
And in the hour of his decease was wrought
A miracle unheard of: at his bedside,
Seen by the Czar alone, appeared a being
Exceeding bright, with whom Feodor spake,
And he addressed him as great Patriarch—
And all around him were possessed with fear,
Musing upon the vision sent from Heaven,
Since the bless'd Patriarch was absent from
The chamber of the Czar. And when he died

The palace was with holy fragrance filled,
And like the sun his countenance shone forth—
Never again shall we see such a czar—
Oh, horrible, appalling woe! We have sinned,
We have angered God; we have chosen for our
Ruler a czar's assassin.

GRIGORY.                    Honored father, long
  Have I desired to ask thee of the death
  Of young Dimitry, the Czarevitch; thou,
  'Tis said, wast then at Uglich.

PIMEN.                              Ay, my son,
  I well remember. God it was who led me
  To witness that ill deed, that bloody sin.
  I at that time was sent to distant Uglich
  Upon some mission. I arrived at night.
  Next morning, at the hour of holy mass,
  I heard upon a sudden a bell toll;
  'Twas the alarm bell. Then a cry, an uproar;
  Men rushing to the court of the Czarina.
  Thither I haste, and there had flocked already
  All Uglich. There I see: the young Czarevitch
  Lies slaughtered, the queen mother in a swoon
  Bowed over him, the nurse in her despair
  Wailing; and then the maddened people drag
  The treacherous nurse away. Now there appears
  Suddenly in their midst, wild, pale with rage,
  That Judas, Bityagovsky. "There's the villain!"
  The raging mob cries out, and in a trice
  He is out of sight. Straightway the people rushed
  At the three fleeing murderers; they seized
  The hiding miscreants and led them up
  To the child's corpse, yet warm; when lo! a
  Marvel—the lifeless little one began to tremble!
  "Confess!" the people thundered; and in terror
  Beneath the ax the villains did confess—
  And named Boris.

GRIGORY.            When this befell, how old
  Was the poor boy?

PIMEN.                Full seven years; and now
  (Since then ten years have passed—nay, more—
      twelve years)
  He would have been of the same age as thou,

And would have reigned; but God deemed otherwise.
This is the lamentable tale wherewith
My chronicle doth end; since then I scarce
Have meddled in the world's affairs. Good brother,
Thou hast acquired the precious art of writing;
To thee I hand my task. In hours exempt
From the soul's exercise, do thou record,
And without sophistry, all things whereto
Thou shalt in life be witness: war and peace,
The sway of kings, the holy miracles
Of saints, all prophecies and heavenly omens —
For me 'tis time to rest and quench my lamp —
But hark! the matin bell. Bless, Lord, thy servants!
Hand me my crutch.

(Exit.)

GRIGORY.           Boris, Boris, before thee
All tremble; none dares even to remind thee
Of what befell the hapless child; meanwhile
In his dark cell a hermit doth set down
A stern indictment of thee. Thou wilt not
Escape the judgment even of this world,
As thou wilt not escape the doom of God.


## BESIDE THE MONASTERY WALL*

GRIGORY *and a* WICKED MONK


GRIGORY. Oh, what a weariness is our poor life,
What misery! Day comes, day goes, and ever
One sees, one hears but the same thing; one sees
Only black cassocks, hears only the bell.
Yawning by day you wander, wander, nothing
To do; you doze; the whole night long till daylight
The poor monk lies awake; and when in sleep
You lose yourself, black dreams disturb the soul;
Glad that they sound the bell, that with a crutch
They rouse you. No, I will not suffer it!

* This scene was omitted by Pushkin from the published text
of the play. Here the poet uses a trochaic meter, not followed by
the translator.

I cannot! I will jump this wall and run!
The world is great; I'll take the open road;
They'll hear of me no more.

MONK.                              Truly your life
Is but a sorry one, ye hot-blooded
And wild young monks!

GRIGORY.                          Would that the Khan again
Assaulted us, or Lithuania
Once more rose up in arms! Good! I would then
Cross swords with them! Or what if the Czarevitch
Should suddenly arise from out the grave,
Should cry, "Where are ye, children, faithful servants?
Help me against Boris, against my murderer!
Seize my foe, bring him to me!"

MONK.                              Enough, my friend,
Of empty talk. We cannot raise the dead.
No, clearly Fate had something else in store
For the Czarevitch— But hearken: if thy mind
Is set upon a deed, then do it.

GRIGORY.                          What?

MONK. If I were young as thou, if these gray hairs
Had not already streaked my beard— Dost take me?

GRIGORY. Not I.

MONK.          Hearken: our folk are dull of brain,
And credulous, and glad to be amazed
By novelties and marvels. The boyars
Remember Godounov as erst he was,
Peer to themselves; and even now the race
Of the Varangians is loved by all.
Thy years match those of the Czarevitch. If
Thou'rt firm and cunning— Dost take me now?

GRIGORY. I take thee.

MONK.              Well, what say'st thou?

GRIGORY.                                  'Tis resolved!
I am Dimitry, the Czarevitch! I!

MONK. Thy hand, my bold young friend. Thou shalt be Czar!

34

# PALACE OF THE PATRIARCH

PATRIARCH *and* ABBOT *of the Chudov Monastery*

PATRIARCH. And he has run away, Father Abbot?

ABBOT. He ran away, holy Patriarch, three days ago.

PATRIARCH. Accursed rascal! What is his origin?

ABBOT. Of the family of the Otrepyevs, of the lower nobility of Halicz; in his youth he took monastic vows, no one knows where, lived in the Yefimievsky monastery at Suzdal, departed thence, wandered from one monastery to another, finally came to our brethren at Chudov; and I, seeing that he was still young and inexperienced, entrusted him at the outset to Father Pimen, a venerable ancient, kind and humble. And he was very learned, read our chronicles, composed hymns to saints; but, it would seem, this learning did not come to him from the Lord God—

PATRIARCH. Ah, those learned ones! What a thing to say, "I shall be Czar in Moscow." Ah, he is a vessel of the devil! However, it is of no use even to report this to the Czar; why disquiet the sovereign, our father? It will be enough to give information about his flight to Secretary Smitnov or Secretary Yefimiev. What heresy: "I shall be Czar in Moscow!" . . . Catch, catch the tool of the devil, and let him endure perpetual penance in exile at Solovetsky. But indeed—is it not heresy, Father Abbot?

ABBOT. Heresy, holy Patriarch; downright heresy.

# PALACE OF THE CZAR

## TWO COURTIERS

FIRST COURTIER. Where is the sovereign?

SECOND COURTIER.                                   In his
    Bed-chamber, where he is closeted with
    Some magician.

FIRST COURTIER. Ay, that's the kind of intercourse he
    Loves: magicians, sorcerers, and fortune-tellers.
    Ever he seeks to dip into the future,
    Just like some pretty girl. Fain would I know
    What 'tis that he would learn.

SECOND COURTIER.                         Well, here he comes.
    Shall we not question him?

FIRST COURTIER.                         How grim he looks!
                         (*Exeunt.*)

CZAR. (*Enters.*) I have attained the highest power. Six
    Years have I reigned peacefully; but happiness
    Dwells not within my soul. Even so in youth
    We greedily desire the joys of love,
    But scarce have quelled the hunger of the heart
    With momentary pleasure, when we grow
    Cold, weary and oppressed! In vain the wizards
    Promise me length of days, days of dominion
    Untroubled and serene—not power, not life
    Rejoice me; I forebode the wrath of Heaven
    And woe. For me there is no joy. I thought
    To give my people glory and contentment,
    To gain their loyal love by generous gifts,
    But I have put away that empty hope;
    The living power is hateful to the mob—
    Only the dead they love. We are but fools
    When our heart shakes because the people clap
    Or cry out fiercely. When our land was stricken
    By God with famine, perishing in torments
    The people uttered moan. I opened to them
    The granaries, I scattered gold among them,
    Found labor for them; yet for all my pains
    They cursed me! Next, a fire consumed their homes;

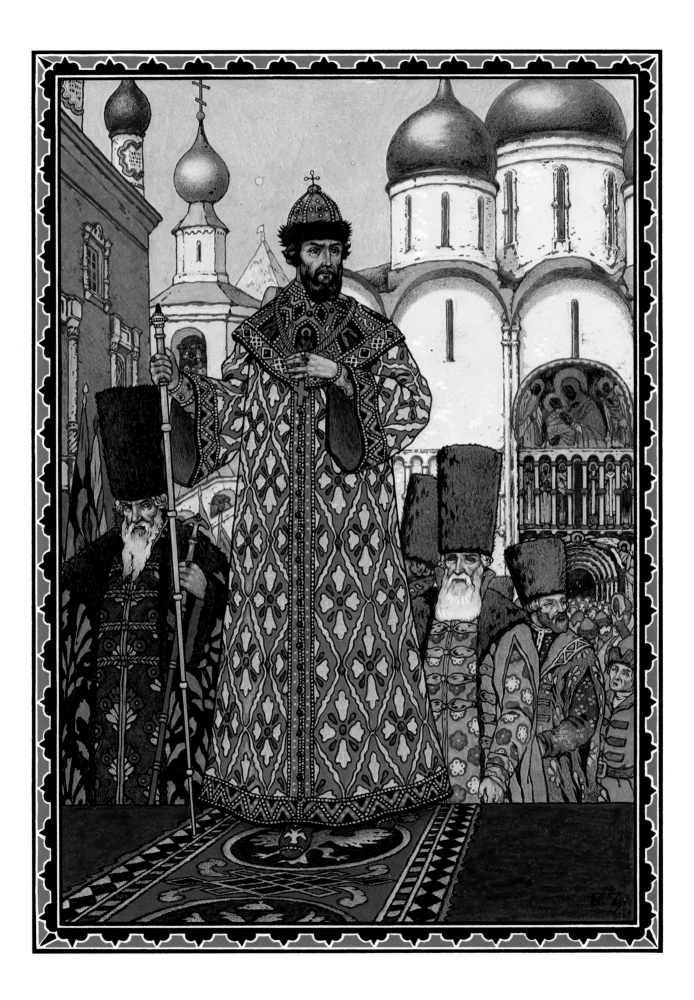

I built for them new dwellings; then forsooth
They blamed me for the fire! Such is the mob,
Such is its judgment! Seek its love, indeed!
I thought within my family to find
Solace; I thought to make my daughter happy
By wedlock. Like a tempest, Death took off
Her bridegroom—and at once a stealthy rumor
Pronounced me guilty of my daughter's grief—
Me, me, the hapless father! Whoso dies,
I am the secret murderer of all;
Feodor's end I hastened, 'twas I poisoned
My sister-queen, the nun—'twas ever I!
Ah! now I feel it; naught can give us peace
Mid worldly cares, nothing save only conscience!
When clear, she triumphs over wickedness,
Over dark slander; but if she be found
To have a single stain, then misery!
With what a deadly sore the soul doth smart;
The heart, with venom filled, beats like a hammer
And dins reproach into the buzzing ears;
The head is spinning, nausea tortures one,
And bloody boys revolve before the eyes;
And one would flee, but refuge there is none!
Oh, pity him whose conscience is unclean!

## TAVERN ON THE LITHUANIAN FRONTIER

MISAIL *and* VARLAAM, *wandering monks;*
GRIGORY *in secular attire;* HOSTESS

HOSTESS. With what shall I regale you, my reverend sirs?

VARLAAM. With what God sends, little hostess. Is there no wine?

HOSTESS. As if that were possible, my fathers! I will bring it at once.

(*Exit.*)

MISAIL. Why so glum, comrade? Here is that very Lithuanian frontier which thou didst so wish to reach.

GRIGORY. Until I am in Lithuania, I shall not be content.

VARLAAM. What is it that makes thee so fond of Lithuania? Here are we, Father Misail and I, sinner that I am, now that we have escaped from the monastery, nothing matters to us. Lithuania, Russia, a whistle, a psaltery? It is all one to us, if only there is wine. And here it is!

MISAIL. Well said, Father Varlaam.

HOSTESS. (*Enters.*)
There you are, my fathers. Drink, and may it do you good.

MISAIL. Thanks, my good friend. God bless thee. (*The monks drink.* VARLAAM *trolls a ditty: "Ah, sweetheart, sweetheart mine, show me those eyes of thine." To* GRIGORY.) Why dost not join in the song? Why dost not join in the drinking?

GRIGORY. I don't wish to.

MISAIL. Everyone to his liking—

VARLAAM. But a tipsy man's in Heaven, Father Misail! Let us drink a glass to our hostess. (*Sings: "Show those eyes of thine."*) Still, Father Misail, when I am drinking, then I don't like sober men; tipsiness is one thing—but pride quite another. One who would live as we do, is welcome. If not—then take thyself off; away with thee; a clown is no companion for a priest.

GRIGORY. Drink, and keep thy thoughts to thyself, Father Varlaam!* I too sometimes know how to speak well.

VARLAAM. But why should I keep my thoughts to myself?

MISAIL. Let him alone, Father Varlaam.

VARLAAM. But what sort of a fasting man is he? Of his own accord he attached himself as a companion to us; no one knows who he is, no one knows whence he comes—and yet he gives himself grand airs. (*Drinks and sings: "A young monk took orders."*)

* They speak in rhymed proverbs.

39

GRIGORY. (*To* HOSTESS.) Whither leads this road?

HOSTESS. To Lithuania, my provider, to the Luyov mountains.

GRIGORY. And is it far to the Luyov mountains?

HOSTESS. Not far; you might get there by evening, but for the Czar's frontier guards, and the officers of the watch.

GRIGORY. What? Guards! What does it mean?

HOSTESS. Someone has escaped from Moscow, and orders have been given to detain and search everyone.

GRIGORY. (*Aside.*) Here's a pretty mess!

VARLAAM. Hallo, comrade! Thou'rt making up to the hostess. To be sure thou wantest no vodka, but a young woman. All right, brother, all right! Everyone has his own ways, and Father Misail and I have only one care—we drink to the bottom, we drink; turn the glass upside down, and knock on the bottom.

MISAIL. Well said, Father Varlaam.

GRIGORY. (*To* HOSTESS.) Whom do they want? Who escaped from Moscow?

HOSTESS. God knows; a thief perhaps, a robber. But here even good folks are plagued now. And what will come of it? Nothing. They'll not catch a hair of the devil; as if there were no other road into Lithuania than the highway! Just turn to the left from here, then through the pine wood follow the footpath as far as the chapel on the Chekansky brook, and then straight across the marsh to Khlopino, and thence to Zakharievo, and there any child will guide you to the Luyov mountains. The only good of these officers is to plague passersby and rob us poor folk. (*A noise is heard.*) What's that? Ah, there they are, curse them! They are going their rounds.

GRIGORY. Hostess! is there another room in the cottage?

HOSTESS. No, my dear; I should be glad myself to hide. But they are only pretending to go their rounds; but give them wine and bread, and Heaven knows what—May they choke, the accursed ones! May—

(*Enter* OFFICERS.)

OFFICERS. Good health to you, hostess!

HOSTESS. You are very welcome, dear guests.

AN OFFICER. (*To another.*) Ha, there's drinking going on here; we shall get something here. (*To the* MONKS.) Who are you?

VARLAAM. We—are God's old men, humble monks; we are going from village to village, and collecting Christian alms for the monastery.

OFFICER. (*To* GRIGORY.) And thou?

MISAIL. Our comrade.

GRIGORY. A layman from the suburb; I have conducted the old men as far as the frontier; from here I am going to my own home.

MISAIL. So thou hast changed thy mind?

GRIGORY. (*Sotto voce.*) Hold thy tongue.

OFFICER. Hostess, bring some more wine, and we will drink here a little and talk a little with these old men.

SECOND OFFICER. (*Sotto voce.*) Yon lad, it appears, is poor; there's nothing to be got out of him; on the other hand, the old men—

FIRST OFFICER. Be silent; we shall come to them presently—Well, my fathers, how goes it?

VARLAAM. Badly, son, badly! The Christians have now turned stingy; they love their money; they hide their money. They give little to God. A great sin has come upon the peoples of the earth. All

41

men have become traders and publicans; they think of worldly wealth, not of the salvation of the soul. You walk and walk; you beg and beg; sometimes in three days begging will not bring you three half-pence. What a sin! A week goes by; another week; you look into your bag, and there is so little in it that you are ashamed to show yourself at the monastery. What are you to do? From very sorrow you drink away what is left; a real calamity! Ah, it is bad! It seems our last days have come—

HOSTESS. (*Weeps.*) God pardon and save us!
(*During the course of* VARLAAM'S *speech the* FIRST OFFICER *was watching* MISAIL *significantly.*)

FIRST OFFICER. Alexis! hast thou the Czar's edict with thee?

SECOND OFFICER. I have it.

FIRST OFFICER. Hand it over.

MISAIL. Why art thou staring at me?

FIRST OFFICER. This is why; from Moscow there has fled a certain wicked heretic—Grishka Otrepyev. Hast thou heard this?

MISAIL. I have not.

OFFICER. Not heard it? Very good. And the Czar has ordered to catch and hang the fugitive heretic. Dost thou know this?

MISAIL. I do not.

OFFICER. (*To* VARLAAM.) Dost know how to read?

VARLAAM. In my youth I knew how, but I have forgotten.

OFFICER. (*To* MISAIL.) And thou?

MISAIL. God has not given me wisdom.

OFFICER. Here's the Czar's edict for thee.

MISAIL. What do I want it for?

OFFICER. It seems to me that this fugitive heretic, thief, swindler, is—thou.

MISAIL. I? Good gracious! What art thou talking of?

OFFICER. Stay! Bar the doors. We shall soon get at the truth at once.

HOSTESS. O the cursèd tormentors! Even an old man they won't leave in peace!

OFFICER. Which of you here can read?

GRIGORY. (Comes forward.) I can read!

OFFICER. Oh, indeed! And who taught thee?

GRIGORY. Our sacristan.

OFFICER. (Gives him the edict.) Read it aloud.

GRIGORY. (Reads.) "Grigory, of the family of Otrepyev, an unworthy monk of the Chudov Monastery, has fallen into heresy, and, instructed by the devil, has dared to stir up the holy brotherhood with all manner of temptations and lawlessness. And, according to information, it appears that he, the accursed Grishka, has fled to the Lithuanian frontier."

OFFICER. (To MISAIL.) How can it be anyone but thou?

GRIGORY. "And the Czar has commanded to catch him—"

OFFICER. And to hang!

GRIGORY. It does not say here "to hang."

OFFICER. Thou liest. What is meant is not always put into writing. Read: to catch and to hang.

GRIGORY. "And to hang. And the years of this thief Grishka" (looking at VARLAAM) "are more than

44

fifty, and he is of medium height; he has a bald head, a gray beard, a fat belly."

(*All look at* VARLAAM.)

FIRST OFFICER. My lads! Here is Grishka! Hold him! bind him! What a surprise!

VARLAAM. (*Snatching the paper.*) Hands off, you dogs! What sort of a Grishka am I? What! fifty years old, gray beard, fat belly! No, brother. You're too young to play tricks on me. I have not read for a long time and I find it hard to make out, but I shall manage to make it out, as it's a hanging matter. (*Spells it out.*) "And his age twenty." Why, brother, where does it say fifty? Do you see—twenty?

SECOND OFFICER. Yes, I remember, twenty; even so it was told us.

FIRST OFFICER. (*To* GRIGORY.) Then, evidently you are a joker, brother.
(*During the reading* GRIGORY *stands with downcast head, and his hand in his bosom.*)

VARLAAM. (*Continues.*) "And in stature he is small, his chest is broad, one arm is shorter than the other, has blue eyes, red hair, a wart on his cheek, another on his forehead." Then is it not thou, my friend? (GRIGORY *suddenly draws a dagger; all give way before him; he dashes through the window.*)

OFFICERS. Hold him! Hold him!

(*All run in disorder.*)


# MOSCOW. SHUISKY'S HOUSE

(*Supper*)

SHUISKY, PUSHKIN, MANY GUESTS


SHUISKY. More wine! (*He rises; all rise after him.*)
   Now, my dear guests. The final jug!
   Boy, read the prayer.

45

BOY.                          Lord of the heavens, who art
     Eternally and everywhere, accept
     The prayer of us thy servants. For our monarch,
     By thee appointed, for our pious Czar,
     The autocrat of Christendom, we pray.
     Preserve him in the palace, on the field
     Of battle, on his nightly couch; grant to him
     Victory o'er his foes; from sea to sea
     May he be glorified; may all his house
     Blossom with health, and may its precious branches
     O'ershadow all the earth; to us, his slaves,
     May he, as heretofore, be generous,
     Gracious, long-suffering, and may the founts
     Of his unfailing wisdom flow for us;
     Raising the royal cup, Lord of the heavens,
     For this we pray.

SHUISKY. (*Drinks.*) Long live our mighty sovereign!
     Farewell, dear guests. I thank you that ye scorned
     Not my bread and salt. Good-bye, and slumber well.
     (*Exeunt* GUESTS: *he conducts them to the door.*)

PUSHKIN. They've left at last; indeed, Prince Vassily
     Ivanovich, I began to think that we should not
     succeed in getting any private talk.

SHUISKY. (*To the* SERVANTS.) You there, why do you
     stand gaping? Always eavesdropping on the mas-
     ters! Clear the table, and then be off.
                         (*Exeunt* SERVANTS.)
                         What is it, Afanasy
     Mikhailovich?

PUSHKIN.          Marvels will never cease!
     A messenger from Cracow came today
     Sent by my nephew, young Gavrila Pushkin.

SHUISKY. Well?

PUSHKIN.          'Tis strange news my nephew writes.
     The son of Czar Ivan the Terrible— But stay—
                    (*Goes to the door and examines it.*)
     The royal boy slain by Boris's order—

SHUISKY. But these are no new tidings.

46

PUSHKIN.                              Wait a little;
  Dimitry lives.

SHUISKY.          So that's it! News indeed!
  Dimitry living! Really marvelous!
  And is that all?

PUSHKIN.              Pray listen to the end;
  Whoe'er he be, whether he be Dimitry
  Rescued, or else some spirit in his shape,
  Some daring rogue, some insolent pretender,
  In any case Dimitry has appeared.

SHUISKY. It cannot be.

PUSHKIN.              Pushkin himself beheld him
  When first he reached the court, and through the
  Ranks of Lithuanian courtiers went straight
  Into the secret chamber of the king.

SHUISKY. What kind of man? Whence comes he?

PUSHKIN.                              No one knows.
  'Tis known that he was Wisniowiecki's servant;
  That to a ghostly father on a bed
  Of sickness he disclosed himself; possessed
  Of this strange secret, his proud magnate nursed
  Him, from his sick bed upraised him, and
  Straightway took him to Sigismund.

SHUISKY.                              And what say men
  Of this bold fellow?

PUSHKIN.              They say he is wise,
  Affable, cunning, pleasing to all men.
  He has bewitched the fugitives from Moscow,
  The Catholic priests see eye to eye with him.
  The king caresses him, and, it is said,
  Has promised help.

SHUISKY.              All this is such a medley
  That my head whirls. Brother, beyond all doubt
  This man is a pretender, but the danger
  Is, I confess, not slight. This is grave news!
  And if it reach the people, then there'll be
  A mighty tempest.

PUSHKIN.                    Such a storm that hardly
    Will Czar Boris contrive to keep the crown
    Upon his clever head; and losing it
    Will get but his deserts! He governs us
    As did the Czar Ivan of evil memory.
    What profits it that public executions
    Have ceased, that we no longer are impaled
    And dripping blood sing hymns to Jesus Christ;
    That we no more are burnt on public squares,
    Or that the Czar no longer with his scepter
    Rakes in the coals? Have we any assurance
    Of our poor lives? Each day disgrace awaits us;
    The dungeon or Siberia, cowl or fetters,
    And then in some lost nook at last starvation,
    Or else the halter. Where are the most renowned
    Of all our houses, where the Sitsky princes,
    Where are the Shestunovs, where the Romanovs,
    Hope of our fatherland? Imprisoned, tortured,
    In exile. Do but wait, and a like fate
    Will soon be thine. Think of it! Here at home,
    We are beset, as if by foreign foes,
    By treacherous slaves—these spies are ever ready
    For base betrayal, thieves bribed by the State.
    We hang upon the word of the first servant
    Whom we may choose to punish. Then he bethought
    Him to bind the peasant to the land he tilled,
    Forbidding change of masters, so that thus
    The masters too are bound. Do not dismiss
    An idler. Willy nilly, thou must feed him!
    Presume not to entice a serf away
    From his old master, or you'll find yourself
    In the court's clutches— Was such an evil heard of
    When Czar Ivan was reigning? Are the people
    Now better off? Ask them. Let the Pretender
    But promise them the old free right of transfer,
    Then there'll be sport.

SHUISKY.                    Thou'rt right; but be advised;
    Of this, of all things, for a time we'll speak
    No word.

PUSHKIN.    Assuredly, keep thine own counsel.
    Thou art—a person of discretion; always
    I speak with thee most gladly; and if aught
    At any time disturbs me, I endure not
    To keep it from thee; and, in truth, thy mead

48

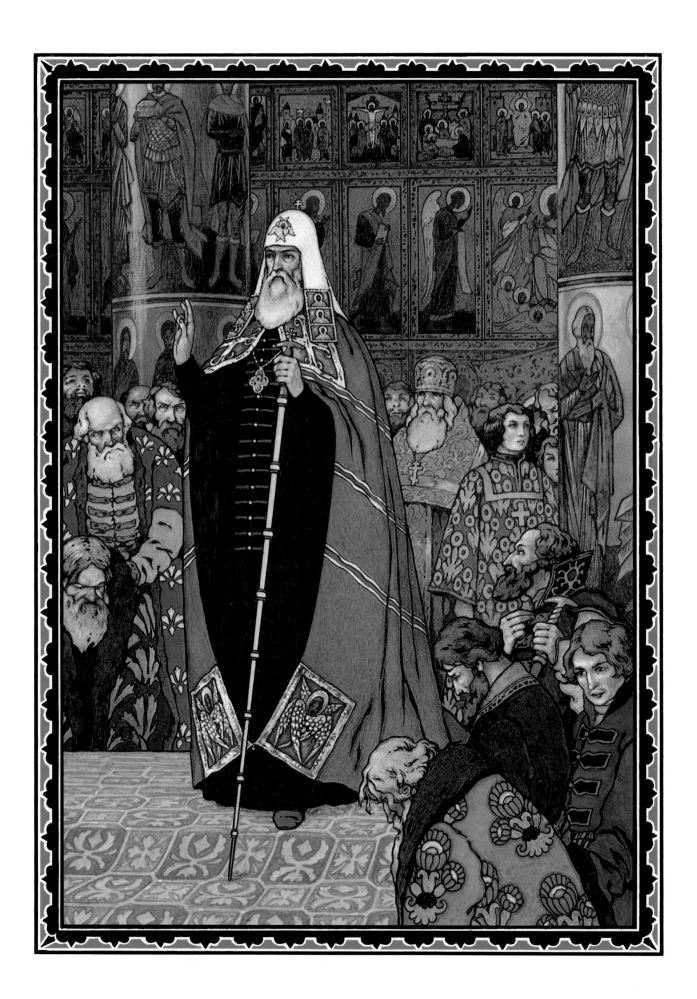

And velvet ale today have so untied
My tongue . . . Farewell then, prince.

SHUISKY.                       Brother, farewell.
Farewell, my brother, till we meet again.
(He escorts PUSHKIN out.)


# PALACE OF THE CZAR

THE CZAREVITCH *is drawing a map;* THE CZAREVNA;
THE NURSE OF THE CZAREVNA

XENIA. (*Kisses a portrait.*) Sweet bridegroom, comely
prince, not to me wast thou given, not to thy af-
fianced bride, but to a dark grave in a strange
land. Never shall I take comfort, ever shall I weep
for thee.

NURSE. Eh, Czarevna! a maiden weeps as the dew
falls; the sun will rise, will dry the dew. Thou wilt
have another bridegroom—and handsome and affable. My charming child, thou wilt learn to love
him, thou wilt forget thy prince.

XENIA. Nay, nurse, I will be true to him even in death.
(BORIS enters.)

CZAR. What, Xenia? What, my sweet one? In thy
Girlhood already a woe-stricken widow, ever
Bewailing thy dead bridegroom! Fate forbade me
To be the author of thy bliss. Perchance
I angered Heaven; it was not mine to compass
Thy happiness. Innocent one, for what
Art thou a sufferer? and thou, my son,
With what art thou employed? What's this?

FEODOR.                          A map
Of all the land of Muscovy; our czardom
From end to end. Here you see: there is Moscow,
There Novgorod, there Astrakhan. Here lies
The sea, here the dense forest tract of Perm,
And there Siberia.

CZAR.                    And what is this
   Which makes a winding pattern here?

FEODOR.                                    That is
   The Volga.

CZAR.          Very good! Here's the sweet fruit
   Of learning. One can view as from the clouds
   Our whole dominion at a glance; its frontiers,
   Its towns, its rivers. Study, son; 'tis science
   That teaches us more swiftly than experience,
   Our life being so brief. Someday, and soon
   Perchance, the lands which thou so cunningly
   Today hast drawn on paper, all will come
   Under thy hand. Then study; and more clearly,
   More steadily wilt thou see, son, before thee
   The sovereign task.
                         (SEMYON GODOUNOV enters.)
                      But there comes Godounov
   Bringing reports to me. (To XENIA.) Go to thy
   Chamber, dearest; farewell, my child; God
   Comfort thee.
                         (Exeunt XENIA and NURSE.)
   What news hast thou for me, Semyon Nikitich?

SEMYON G. Today at dawn the butler of Prince Shuisky
   And Pushkin's servant brought me information.

CZAR. Well?

SEMYON G. In the first place, Pushkin's man deposed
   That yestermorn came to his house from Cracow
   A courier, who within an hour was sent
   Without a letter back.

CZAR.                         Arrest the courier.

SEMYON G. Some are already sent to overtake him.

CZAR. And what of Shuisky?

SEMYON G.                    Last night he entertained
   His friends: the Buturlins, both Miloslavskys,
   And Saltykov, with Pushkin and some others.
   They parted late. Pushkin alone remained
   Closeted with his host and talked with him
   And at some length.

CZAR. For Shuisky send forthwith.

SEMYON G. Sire, he is here already.

CZAR. Call him hither.
(*Exit* SEMYON GODOUNOV.)
Dealings with Lithuania? What means this?
I like not the rebellious race of Pushkins,
Nor must I trust in Shuisky, who's evasive,
But bold and wily—
(*Enter* SHUISKY.)
Prince, a word with thee.
But thou thyself, it seems, hast business with me,
And I would listen first to thee.

SHUISKY. Yea, sire;
It is my duty to convey to thee
Grave news.

CZAR. I listen.

SHUISKY. (*Sotto voce, pointing to* FEODOR.)
But, sire—

CZAR. The Czarevitch
May learn whate'er Prince Shuisky knoweth. Speak.

SHUISKY. My liege, from Lithuania there have come
Tidings to us—

CZAR. Are they not those same tidings
Which yestereve a courier bore to Pushkin?

SHUISKY. Nothing is hidden from him! Sire, I thought
Thou knew'st not yet this secret.

CZAR. Let not that
Trouble thee, prince; I fain would match thy news
With what I know; else we shall never learn
The actual truth.

SHUISKY. I know this only, sire:
In Cracow a pretender hath appeared;
The king and nobles back him.

CZAR. What say they?
And who is this pretender?

SHUISKY.                         I know not.

CZAR. But wherein is he dangerous?

SHUISKY.                              Verily
    Thy power, my liege, is firm; by vigilance,
    Grace, bounty, thou hast won the filial love
    Of all thy slaves; but thou thyself dost know
    The mob is thoughtless, changeable, rebellious,
    Credulous, lightly given to vain hope,
    Obedient to each momentary impulse,
    To truth deaf and indifferent; it doth feed
    On fables; shameless boldness pleaseth it.
    So, if this unknown vagabond should cross
    The Lithuanian border, Dimitry's name
    Raised from the grave will gain him a whole crowd
    Of fools.

CZAR. Dimitry's? What? That child's? Dimitry's?
    Withdraw, my son.

SHUISKY.                 He flushed; there'll be a storm!

FEODOR. Suffer me, sire—

CZAR.                         Impossible, Czarevitch;
    Go, go!                           (*Exit* FEODOR.)
            Dimitry's name!

SHUISKY.                   Then he knew nothing.

CZAR. Listen: take steps this very hour that Russia
    Be fenced by barriers from Lithuania;
    That not a single soul pass o'er the border,
    That not a hare run o'er to us from Poland,
    Nor crow fly here from Cracow. Off!

SHUISKY.                         I go.

CZAR. Stay! Is it not the truth that this report
    Is artfully contrived? Hast ever heard
    That dead men have arisen from their graves
    To question czars, legitimate czars, appointed,
    Acclaimed by all the people, yea, and crowned
    By the great Patriarch? Should one not laugh?
    Eh? What? Why laugh'st thou not thereat?

54

SHUISKY.                                        I, sire?

CZAR. Hark, Prince Vassily; when I learned this child
    Had been—this child had somehow lost its life,
    'Twas thou I sent to search the matter out.
    Now by the Cross, by God I do adjure thee,
    Declare to me the truth upon thy conscience:
    Didst recognize the slaughtered boy, or didst
    Thou find another? Answer.

SHUISKY.                              Sire, I swear—

CZAR. Nay, Shuisky, swear not, but reply; was it
    Indeed Dimitry?

SHUISKY.            He.

CZAR.                Consider, prince.
    I promise clemency; I will not punish
    With vain disgrace a lie that's of the past.
    But if thou cheat me now, then by my own
    Son's head I swear—an ill fate shall befall thee,
    Such punishment that Czar Ivan himself
    Shall shudder in his grave with horror of it.

SHUISKY. In punishment no terror lies; the terror
    Doth lie in thy disfavor; in thy presence
    Dare I use cunning? Could I have been so blind
    That I then failed to recognize Dimitry?
    Three days in the cathedral did I visit
    His corpse, escorted thither by all Uglich.
    Around him thirteen bodies lay of those
    Slain by the people, and in them corruption
    Already had set in perceptibly.
    But lo! the childish face of the Czarevitch
    Was bright and fresh and still as though he slept;
    The deep gash had congealed not, nor the lines
    Of his face even altered. No, my liege,
    There is no doubt; Dimitry's in his grave.

CZAR. (*Calmly.*) Enough, withdraw.
                                        (*Exit* SHUISKY.)
                    I choke! Let me draw breath!
    I felt it; all my blood surged to my face,
    And heavily receded. So that's why
    For thirteen years together I have dreamed

55

Ever about the murdered child. Yes, yes—
'Tis that!—now I perceive. But who is he,
My terrible antagonist? Who is it
Opposeth me? An empty name, a shadow.
Can but a ghost tear from my back the purple,
A hollow sound make beggars of my children?
This is pure madness! What is there to fear?
Blow on this phantom—and it is no more.
So, I am fast resolved; I'll show no sign
Of fear, but let no trifle be ignored.
Ah! heavy art thou, crown of Monomakh!

# HOUSE OF WISNIOWIECKI

## (Cracow)

THE PRETENDER *and* FATHER CZERNIKOWSKI, *a Jesuit*

PRETENDER. Nay, father, it will not be hard. I know
   The spirit of my people; piety
   With them is not extreme, their Czar's example
   To them is sacred. And their tolerance
   Makes them indifferent. I warrant you,
   Before two years my people all, and all
   The Northern Church, will recognize the power
   Of Peter's Vicar.

JESUIT.                    May Saint Ignatius aid thee
    When other times arrive. Meanwhile, Czarevitch,
    Hide in thy soul the seed of heavenly grace;
    Religious duty bids us oft dissemble
    Before the impious world; the people judge
    Thy words, thy deeds; God only sees thy motives.

PRETENDER. Amen. Who's there?

                                        (*Enter a* SERVANT.)
                        Say that we will receive them.
    (*The doors are opened; enter a crowd of* RUSSIANS
        *and* POLES.)
    Comrades! Tomorrow we depart from Cracow.
    Mniszech, with thee for three days in Sambor
    I'll stay. I know thy hospitable castle
    Both shines in splendid stateliness, and glories
    In its young mistress. There I hope to see
    Charming Maryna. And ye, my friends, ye, Russians
    And Lithuanians, ye who have upraised
    Fraternal banners 'gainst a common foe,
    Against mine enemy, yon crafty villain,
    Ye sons of Slavs, speedily will I lead
    Your dread battalions to the longed-for conflict.
    But soft! Methinks among you I descry
    New faces.

PUSHKIN. They have come to beg for sword
    And service with your Grace.

PRETENDER.                          . Welcome, my lads.
    Come hither, friends. But tell me, Pushkin, who
    Is this fine youth?

PUSHKIN.           Prince Kurbsky.

PRETENDER. (*To* KURBSKY.)           A proud name!
    Art kinsman to the hero of Kazan?

KURBSKY. His son.

PRETENDER.        Doth he still live?

60

KURBSKY.                                   Nay, he is dead.

PRETENDER. A noble mind! A man of war and counsel.
    But from the time when he appeared beneath
    The ancient town Olgin with Lithuanians,
    Hardy avenger of his injuries,
    Rumor hath held her tongue concerning him.

KURBSKY. My father passed the remnant of his life
    On lands bestowed upon him by Bathory;
    There, in Volhynia, a peaceful hermit,
    Sought consolation for himself in learning;
    But quiet labor did not comfort him;
    He ne'er forgot the home of his young days,
    And to the end pined for it.

PRETENDER.                          Hapless chieftain!
    How brightly shone the dawn of his resounding
    And stormy life! Glad am I, noble knight,
    That now in thee his blood is reconciled
    To his own country. Faults of fathers must not
    Be called to mind. Peace to their graves. Approach;
    Give me thy hand! Is it not strange? The son
    Of Kurbsky to the throne is leading—whom?
    Whom but Ivan's own son? All favors me;
    People and fate alike. Say, who art thou?

A POLE. Sobanski, a free noble.

PRETENDER.                          Praise and honor
    Attend thee, child of liberty. Give him
    A third of his full pay beforehand— Who
    Are these? On them I recognize the garb
    Of my own country. These are ours.

KHRUSHCHOV. (*Bows low.*)                Yea, sire,
    Our father; we are thralls of thine, devoted
    And persecuted; we have fled from Moscow,
    Disgraced, to thee our Czar, and for thy sake
    Are ready to lay down our lives; our corpses
    Shall be for thee steps to the royal throne.

PRETENDER. Take heart, innocent sufferers. Only let me
    Reach Moscow, and, once there, Boris shall settle
    Some scores with me and you. What news of
    Moscow?*

KHRUSHCHOV. As yet all there is quiet. But already
    The folk have got to know that the Czarevitch
    Was saved; already everywhere is read
    Thy proclamation. All are waiting for thee.
    Not long ago Boris sent two boyars
    To meet their death merely because in secret
    They drank thy health.

PRETENDER.              O hapless, good boyars!
    But blood for blood! and woe to Godounov!
    What do they say of him?

KHRUSHCHOV.           He has withdrawn
    Into his gloomy palace. He is grim
    And somber. Executions loom ahead.
    But sickness gnaws him. Hardly hath he strength
    To drag himself along, and—it is thought—
    His last hour is already not far off.

PRETENDER. A speedy death I wish him, as becomes
    A great-souled foe to wish. If not, then woe
    To the miscreant! And whom doth he intend
    To name as his successor?

KHRUSHCHOV.           He shows not
    His purposes, but it would seem he destines
    Feodor, his young son, to be our czar.

PRETENDER. His reckonings, maybe, will yet prove
    Wrong. And who art thou?

KARELA.          A Cossack; from the Don
    Sent to thee, from the free troops, the brave
    Chieftains of both the upper and lower reaches,

---

* The passage beginning with this last phrase, down to the line ending "will yet prove wrong," appears only in a manuscript draft of the play.

To look upon thy bright and royal eyes,
And tender thee their homage.

PRETENDER.                              Well I knew
The men of Don; I doubted not to see
The Cossack banners in my ranks. We thank
Our army of the Don. Today, we know,
The Cossacks are unjustly persecuted,
Oppressed; but if God grant us to ascend
The throne of our forefathers, as of yore
We will reward our free and faithful Don.

POET. (*Approaches, bowing low, and taking* GRIGORY
    *by the hem of his caftan.*)
Great prince, illustrious offspring of a king!

PRETENDER. What wouldst thou?

POET.                              Condescendingly accept
This poor fruit of my earnest toil.

PRETENDER.                              What see I?
Verses in Latin! Blest a hundredfold
The tie of sword and lyre; the selfsame laurel
Binds them in friendship. I was born beneath
A northern sky, but yet the Latin muse
To me is a familiar voice; I love
The blossoms of Parnassus, I believe
The prophecies of poets. Not in vain
The ecstasy seethes in their flaming breasts;
The deed is hallowed which is glorified
Beforehand by the poets! Approach, friend.
In memory of me accept this gift.
                              (*Gives him a ring.*)
When fate fulfills for me her covenant,
When I assume the crown of my forefathers,
I hope again to hear the measured tones
Of thy sweet voice, and thy inspired lay.
*Musa gloriam coronat, gloriaque musam.*
And so friends, till tomorrow, fare you well.

ALL. Forward! Long live Dimitry! Forward, forward!
Long live Dimitry, the great prince of Moscow!

# CASTLE OF GOVERNOR
# MNISZECH AT SAMBOR*

(*Maryna's dressing room*)

MARYNA, RUZIA (*dressing her*), SERVING-WOMEN

MARYNA. (*Before a mirror.*) Now, is it ready? Canst
  Thou not make haste?

RUZIA. I pray you first to make the difficult choice;
  What will you wear—the necklace made of pearls—
  The emerald crescent?

MARYNA.                    No, my diamond crown.

RUZIA. Splendid! Do you remember that you wore it
  When to the palace you were pleased to go?
  They say that at the ball your gracious highness
  Shone like the sun; men sighed, fair ladies
  Whispered—'twas then that for the first time young
  Chodkiewicz beheld you, he who later shot himself.
  And whosoever looked on you, they say
  That instant fell in love.

MARYNA.                    Make haste! Make haste!

RUZIA. At once. Today your father counts upon you.
  'Twas not for naught the young Czarevitch saw you;
  He could not hide his rapture; wounded is he
  Already; so it only needs to deal him
  A resolute blow, and instantly, my lady,
  He'll be in love with you. 'Tis now a month
  Since, quitting Cracow, heedless of the war
  And the throne of Moscow, he has feasted here,
  Your guest, enraging Poles alike and Russians.
  Heavens! Shall I yet live to see the day?
  Say you will not, when to his capital
  Dimitry leads the queen of Moscow, say
  You'll not forsake me?

  * This scene was omitted by Pushkin from the published text of
the play. Here the blank verse yields to irregular rhymed lines.

MARYNA                    Dost thou truly think
  I shall be queen?

RUZIA.                    Who, if not you? Who here
  Dares to compare in beauty with my mistress?
  The race of Mniszech never yet has yielded
  To any. You in intellect are past
  All praise—happy the suitor whom your glance
  Honors with its regard, who wins your heart—
  Whoe'er he be, be he our king, the dauphin
  Of France, or even this your poor Czarevitch,
  Though who he is, and whence he comes,
  God knows!

MARYNA. He's the Czar's son, as all the world admits.

RUZIA. And yet last winter he was but a servant
  In Wisniowiecki's house.

MARYNA.                    He was in hiding.

RUZIA. I do not question it: but do you know
  What people say about him? That perhaps
  He is a deacon run away from Moscow,
  In his own parish a notorious rogue.

MARYNA. What nonsense!

RUZIA.                    Oh, I do not credit it!
  I only say he ought to bless his fate
  That you have so preferred him to the others.

SERVING-WOMAN. (*Runs in.*) The guests have come
  Already.

MARYNA. There, you see;
  You are prepared to chatter on till daybreak.
  Meanwhile I am not dressed—

RUZIA                              Within a moment
  'Twill be quite ready.
                (*The* SERVING-WOMEN *bustle.*)

MARYNA. (*Aside.*)          I must find out all.

## CASTLE OF GOVERNOR MNISZECH
## AT SAMBOR

(*A suite of lighted rooms. Music*)

MNISZECH, WISNIOWIECKI

MNISZECH. With none but my Maryna doth he speak,
   With no one else preoccupied—such doings
   Seem to portend a wedding. Now confess,
   Didst ever think my daughter would be queen?

WISNIOWIECKI. Indeed, a marvel— Mniszech, didst
   Thou think my servant would ascend the throne
   of Moscow?

MNISZECH. And what a girl, look you, is my Maryna.
   I merely hinted to her: "Now, be careful!
   Let not Dimitry slip"—and lo! already
   He is completely tangled in her toils.
      (*The band plays a Polonaise. The* PRETENDER *and*
      MARYNA *advance as the first couple.*)

MARYNA. (*Sotto voce to* DIMITRY.) Tomorrow evening
   At eleven, beside the fountain that is in the
   Linden alley.
                     (*They part. A second couple.*)

CAVALIER. What can Dimitry see in her?

LADY.                                    What say you?
  She is a beauty.

CAVALIER.          Yes, a marble nymph;
  Eyes, lips, devoid of life, without a smile.
                              (*A fresh couple.*)

LADY. He is not handsome, but his looks are pleasing,
  And one can see he is of royal birth.
                              (*A fresh couple.*)

LADY. When will the army march?

CAVALIER.                          When the Czarevitch
  Orders it; we are ready; but 'tis clear
  The lady Mniszech and Dimitry mean
  To keep us prisoners here.

LADY.                          A pleasant durance.

CAVALIER. Truly, if you . . .
                  (*They part; the rooms become empty.*)

MNISZECH.              We old folk dance no longer;
  The gay mazurka lures us not; we press not
  Nor kiss the hands of charmers—ah! my friend,
  I've not forgotten the old pranks! Things now
  Are not what once they were, what once they were!
  Youth, I'll be sworn, is not so bold, nor beauty
  So lively; everything—confess, my friend—
  Has somehow become dull. So let us leave them;
  My comrade, let us go and find a flask
  Of old Hungarian overgrown with mold;
  Let's bid my butler open an old bottle,
  And in a quiet corner, *tête-à-tête*,
  Let's drain a draught, a stream as thick as fat;
  And while we're so engaged, let's think things over.
  Let us go, brother.

WISNIOWIECKI.      Yes, my friend, let's go.

# NIGHT

*(The garden. The fountain)*

PRETENDER. *(Enters.)* Here is the fountain; hither
  Will she come.
  I was not born a coward; I have seen
  Death near at hand, and face to face with death
  My spirit hath not blenched. A life-long dungeon
  Hath threatened me, I have been close pursued,
  And yet my spirit quailed not, and by boldness
  I have escaped captivity. But what
  Is this which now constricts my breath? What means
  This overpowering tremor, or this quivering
  Of tense desire? No, this is fear. All day
  I have been waiting for this meeting, pondering
  On all that I should say to her, how best
  I might enmesh Maryna's haughty mind,
  Calling her queen of Moscow. But the hour
  Has come—and I remember naught, I cannot
  Recall the speeches I have learned by rote;
  Love puts imagination to confusion—
  But something there gleamed suddenly—a rustling;
  Hush—no, it was the moon's deceitful light,
  It was the rustling of the breeze.

MARYNA. *(Enters.)*                Czarevitch!

PRETENDER. 'Tis she. Now all the blood in me
  Stands still.

MARYNA. Dimitry! Is it thou?

PRETENDER.                Bewitching voice!
                     *(Goes to her.)*
  Is it thou, at last? Is it thou I see, alone
  With me, beneath the roof of quiet night?
  How slowly passed the tedious day! How slowly
  The glow of evening died away! How long
  I've waited in the gloom of night!

MARYNA.                              The hours
    Are flitting fast, and time is precious to me.
    I did not grant a meeting here to thee
    To listen to a lover's tender speeches.
    No need of words. I well believe thou lovest;
    But listen; with thy stormy, doubtful fate
    I have resolved to join my own; but one thing,
    Dimitry, I require: I claim that thou
    Disclose to me thy secret hopes, thy plans,
    Even thy fears, that hand in hand with thee
    I may confront life boldly—not in blindness
    Of childlike ignorance, not as the slave
    And plaything of my husband's light desires,
    Thy speechless concubine, but as thy spouse,
    And worthy helpmate of the Czar of Moscow.

PRETENDER. Oh, if it be only for one short hour,
    Forget the cares and troubles of my fate!
    Forget 'tis the Czarevitch whom thou seest
    Before thee. O, behold in me, Maryna,
    A lover, by thee chosen, happy only
    In one look from thee. Listen to the prayers
    Of love! Grant me to utter all wherewith
    My heart is full.

MARYNA.              Prince, this is not the time;
    Thou tarriest, and meanwhile the devotion
    Of thine adherents cooleth. Hour by hour
    Danger becomes more dangerous, difficulties
    More difficult; already dubious rumors
    Are current, novelty already takes
    The place of novelty; and Godounov
    Adopts his measures.

PRETENDER.              What is Godounov?
    Is thy sweet love, my only blessedness,
    Swayed by Boris? Nay, nay. Indifferently
    I now regard his throne, his kingly power.
    Thy love—without it what to me is life,
    And glory's glitter, and the throne of Russia?
    On the far steppe, in a poor mud hut, thou—
    Thou wilt requite me for the kingly crown;
    Thy love—

71

MARYNA.　　　For shame! Forget not, prince, thy high
　　And sacred destiny; thy dignity
　　Should be to thee more dear than all the joys
　　Of life and its allurements. This thou canst not
　　With anything compare. Not to a youth,
　　Enthralled, inflamed to madness by my beauty—
　　But to the heir of Moscow's throne I give
　　My hand in solemn wise, to the Czarevitch
　　Rescued by destiny.

PRETENDER.　　　　　Torture me not,
　　Charming Maryna; say not 'twas my rank
　　And not myself that thou didst choose. Maryna!
　　Thou knowest not how sorely thou dost wound
　　My heart thereby. What if—oh, fearful doubt!—
　　Say, if blind destiny had not assigned me
　　A kingly birth; if I were not indeed
　　Son of Ivan, were not this boy, so long
　　Forgotten by the world—say, then wouldst thou
　　Have loved me?

MARYNA.　　　Thou art Dimitry, and aught else
　　Thou canst not be; it is not possible
　　For me to love another.

PRETENDER.　　　　　Nay! enough—
　　I have no wish to share with a dead body
　　A mistress who belongs to him; I have done
　　With counterfeiting, and will tell the truth.
　　Know, then, that thy Dimitry long ago
　　Perished, was buried—not to rise again;
　　And wouldst thou know what sort of man I am?
　　Well, I will tell thee. I am—a poor monk.
　　Grown weary of monastic servitude,
　　I pondered 'neath the cowl my bold design,
　　Made ready for the world a miracle—
　　And from my cell at last fled to the Cossacks,
　　To their wild hovels; there I learned to handle
　　Both steeds and swords; I showed myself to you,
　　I called myself Dimitry, and deceived
　　The brainless Poles. What say'st thou, proud
　　Maryna? Art thou content with my confession? Why
　　Dost thou keep silence?

MARYNA.                    O shame! O woe is me!
                                              (*Silence.*)

PRETENDER. (*Sotto voce.*) O whither hath a fit of anger
    Led me?
    The happiness devised with so much labor
    I have, perchance, destroyed forever. Madman,
    What have I done? (*Aloud.*) I see thou art ashamed
    Of love not princely; so pronounce on me
    The fatal word; my fate is in thy hands.
    Decide; I wait.
                                    (*Falls on his knees.*)

MARYNA.          Rise, poor impostor! Think'st thou
    To please with genuflections my vain heart,
    As if I were a weak, confiding girl?
    You err, my friend; prone at my feet I've seen
    Knights and counts nobly born; but not for this
    Did I reject their prayers, that a truant monk—

PRETENDER. (*Rises.*) Scorn not the young pretender;
    Noble virtues may lie perchance in him, virtues
    Deserving of Moscow's throne, even of thy
    Priceless hand—

MARYNA. Deserving of a noose, insolent wretch!

PRETENDER. I am to blame; carried away by pride
    I have deceived God and the kings—have lied
    Unto the world; but it is not for thee,
    Maryna, to wreak punishment upon me.
    Before thee I am guiltless, do not doubt it.
    No, I could not deceive thee. Thou to me
    Wast the one sacred being, before thee
    I dared not to dissemble; love alone,
    Love, jealous, blind, constrained me to tell all.

MARYNA. What's that to boast of, madman? Who
    Demanded confession of thee? If thou, a nameless
    Vagrant, couldst wonderfully blind two nations,
    Then at least thou shouldst deserve thy high success,
    And thy bold fraud shouldst have secured, by deep

And lasting secrecy. Say, can I yield
Myself to thee, can I, forgetting rank
And maiden modesty, unite my fate
With thine, when thou thyself impetuously
Dost thus with such simplicity reveal
Thy shame? Because of love he blabbed to me!
I marvel wherefore thou hast not from friendship
Disclosed thyself ere now unto my father,
Or else unto our king from joy, or else
Unto Prince Wisniowiecki from the zeal
Of a devoted servant.

PRETENDER.                    I swear to thee
That thou alone wast able to extort
My heart's confession; I swear to thee that never,
Nowhere, not in the feast, not in the cup
Of folly, not in friendly confidence,
Not 'neath the knife nor tortures of the rack,
Shall my tongue give away these weighty secrets.

MARYNA. Thou swearest! Then I must believe. Believe,
Of course! But may I learn by what thou swearest?
Is it not by the name of God, as suits
The Jesuits' devout adopted son?
Or by thy honor as a high-born knight?
Or, maybe, by the royal word alone
As a king's son? Is it not so? Declare.

PRETENDER. (*Proudly.*) The phantom of the Terrible
Adopted me as his son; from out the grave hath
Named me Dimitry, hath stirred up the nations
Round me, and hath consigned Boris to be my victim.
I am Czarevitch. Enough! 'Twere shame for me
To stoop before a haughty Polish woman.
Farewell forever; the bloody game of war,
The vast cares of my destiny, will stifle,
I hope, the pangs of love. Oh, when the heat
Of shameful passion is o'erspent, how then
Shall I detest thee! Now I leave thee—ruin,
Or else a crown, awaits my head in Russia;
Whether I meet with death as fits a soldier
In honorable fight, or as a miscreant
Upon the public scaffold, thou shalt not

Be my companion, nor shalt share with me
My fate; but it may be thou shalt regret
The destiny thou hast refused.

MARYNA.                                         But what
If I expose beforehand thy bold fraud
To all?

PRETENDER. And dost thou truly think I fear thee?
Will they believe a Polish maiden more
Than Russia's own Czarevitch? Know, proud lady,
That neither king, nor pope, nor nobles trouble
Whether my words be true, whether I be
Dimitry or another. What care they?
But I provide a pretext for dispute
And war; and this is all they need; and thee,
Rebellious one, believe me, they will force
To hold thy peace. Farewell.

MARYNA.                                         Czarevitch, stay!
At last I hear the speech not of a boy,
But of a man. It reconciles me to thee.
Prince, I forget thy mad outburst, and see
Again Dimitry. Listen; now is the time!
Awake; delay no more, lead on thy troops
Quickly to Moscow, purge the Kremlin, take
Thy seat upon the throne of Moscow; then
Send me the nuptial envoy; but, God hears me,
Until thou tread the step ascending to
The throne, until by thee Boris be vanquished,
My ears are deaf to any word of love.

                                                        (*Exit.*)

PRETENDER. No—easier far to strive with Godounov,
Or to play false with courtly Jesuits,
Than with a woman. Deuce take them; they're
Beyond my power. She twists, and coils, and crawls,
Slips out of hand, she hisses, threatens, bites. Ah,
Serpent! Serpent! 'Twas not for nothing that I
Trembled. She well-nigh ruined me; but I'm
Resolved; at daybreak I will put my troops in motion.

76

# THE LITHUANIAN FRONTIER

PRINCE KURBSKY *and* PRETENDER, *both
on horseback.* TROOPS *approach the frontier*

KURBSKY. (*First to reach the frontier.*) There, there it
  Is; there is the Russian frontier!
  Fatherland! Holy Russia! I am thine!
  With scorn from off my clothing now I shake
  The foreign dust, and greedily I drink
  New air; it is my native air. O father,
  Thy soul hath now been solaced; in the grave
  Thy bones, disgraced, thrill with a sudden joy!
  Again doth flash our old ancestral sword,
  This glorious sword—the dread of dark Kazan!
  This good sword—servant of the Czars of Moscow!
  Now will it revel in its feast of slaughter,
  Serving the master whom it trusts.

PRETENDER. (*Rides quietly with bowed head.*) How happy
  Is he, how flushed with gladness and with glory
  His stainless soul! Brave knight, I envy thee!
  The son of Kurbsky, thou in exile nurtured,
  Forgetting all the wrongs borne by thy father,
  Redeeming his transgression in the grave,
  Thou for the son of great Ivan art ready
  To shed thy blood, to give the fatherland
  Its lawful czar. Righteous art thou; thy soul
  Should flame with joy.

KURBSKY.                    And dost not thou likewise
  Rejoice in spirit? There lies our Russia; she
  Is thine, Czarevitch! There thy people's hearts
  Are waiting for thee, there thy Moscow waits,
  Thy Kremlin, thy dominion.

PRETENDER.                    Russian blood,
  O Kurbsky, first must flow! You for the Czar
  Have drawn your swords, you are stainless; but I

Lead you against your brothers; I am summoning
Lithuania against Russia; I am showing
To foes the longed-for way to beauteous Moscow!
But let my sin fall not on me, but thee,
Boris, the regicide! Forward! Set on!

KURBSKY. Forward! Advance! And woe to Godounov.
(*They gallop. The* TROOPS *cross the frontier.*)

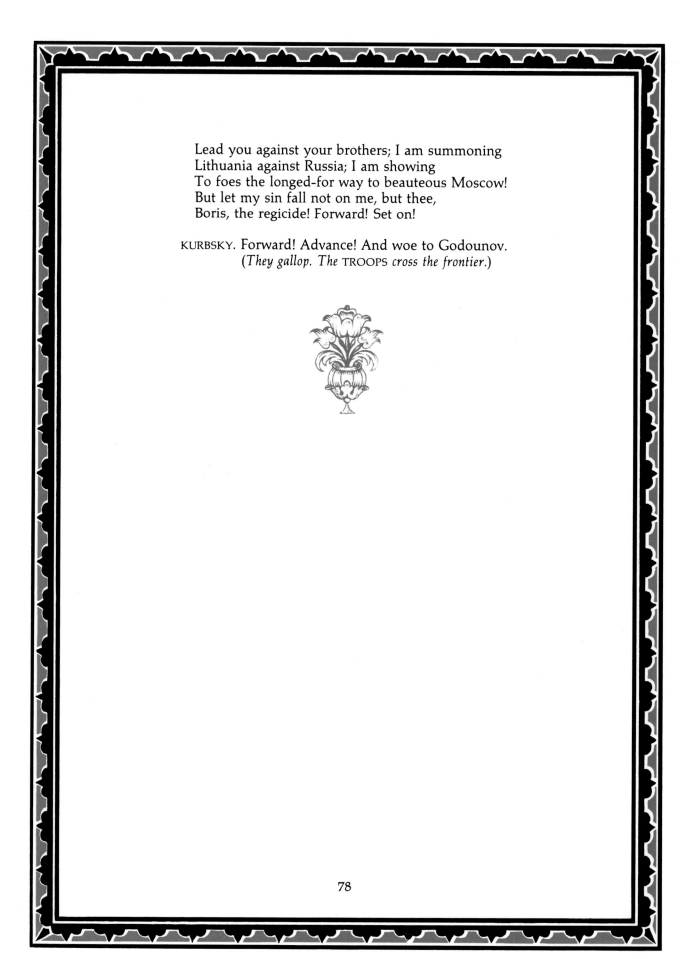

# LE CONSEIL DU TSAR

## THE COUNCIL OF THE CZAR

*(1604)*

THE CZAR, THE PATRIARCH *and* BOYARS

CZAR. Is it possible? An unfrocked monk against us
　　Leads rascal troops, a truant friar dares threaten
　　Our august person! 'Tis time to tame the madman!
　　Go thou forth, Trubetskoy, and thou Basmanov;
　　My zealous governors need help. Chernigov
　　Already by the rebel is besieged;
　　Rescue the town and citizens.

81

BASMANOV.                              Three months
    Shall not pass, sire, ere even rumor's tongue
    Shall cease to speak of the Pretender; caged
    In iron, like a beast from oversea,
    We'll hale him into Moscow, aye, by God.
                              (*Exit with* TRUBETSKOY.)

CZAR. The king of Sweden hath by envoys tendered
    Me his alliance. But we have no need
    To lean on foreign aid; we have enough
    Of our own fighting forces to repel
    The traitors and the Poles. I have refused—
    Shchelkalov! Send to every governor
    An edict that he mount his steed, and press
    The people into service, as of old;
    The servants of the clergy likewise should
    Be pressed into the service. When, of old,
    The land was threatened, of their own free will
    Hermits bore arms; it is not now our wish
    To trouble them; no, let them pray for us;
    Such is the Czar's decree, such the resolve
    Of his boyars. And now a weighty question
    We shall decide; ye know how everywhere
    The insolent Pretender hath sent forth
    His artful rumors; letters everywhere,
    By him distributed, have sowed alarm
    And doubt; seditious whispers to and fro
    Pass in the marketplaces; minds are seething.
    We needs must cool them; gladly would I keep
    From executions, but by what means and how?
    That we will now determine. Holy father,
    Thou first declare thy thought.

PATRIARCH.                          The Blessed One,
    The All-Highest, hath instilled into thy soul,
    Great lord, the breath of kindness and meek
    Patience; thou wishest not perdition for the
    Sinner, thou wilt wait quietly, until delusion
    Shall pass away; for pass away it will,

And truth's eternal sun will dawn on all.
Thy faithful bedesman, one in worldly matters
No able judge, ventures today to offer
His voice to thee. This offspring of the devil,
This unfrocked monk, has well impersonated
Dimitry for the people. Shamelessly
He clothed him with the name of the Czarevitch
As with a stolen vestment. It only needs
To rip it—and he will be put to shame
By his own nakedness. The means thereto
God hath himself supplied. Know, sire, six years
Since then have fled; 'twas in that very year
When to the seat of sovereignty the Lord
Anointed thee—there came to me one evening
A simple shepherd, a venerable old man,
Who told me a strange secret. "In my young days,"
He said, "I lost my sight, and thenceforth knew not
Nor day, nor night, till my old age; in vain
I plied myself with herbs and secret spells;
In vain did I resort in adoration
To the great wonder-workers in the cloisters;
Bathed my dark eyes in vain with healing water
From out the holy wells. The Lord vouchsafed not
Healing to me. Then I lost hope at last,
And grew accustomed to my darkness. Even
Slumber showed not to me things visible,
Only of sounds I dreamed. Once in deep sleep
I hear a childish voice; it speaks to me:
'Arise, grandfather, go to Uglich town,
To the Cathedral of Transfiguration;
There pray over my grave. The Lord is gracious—
And I shall pardon thee.' 'But who art thou?'
I asked the childish voice. 'I'm the Czarevitch
Dimitry, whom the Heavenly Czar hath taken
Into his angel band, and I am now
A mighty wonder-worker. Go, old man.'
I woke, and pondered. What is this? Maybe
God will in very deed vouchsafe to me
Belated healing. I will go. I bend

My footsteps to the distant road. I reach
Uglich, repair unto the holy minster,
Hear mass, and, zealous soul aglow, I weep
Sweetly, as if the blindness from mine eyes
Were flowing out in tears. And when the people
Began to leave, to my grandson I said:
'Lead me, Ivan, to where the young Czarevitch
Lies buried.' The boy led me—and I scarce
Had shaped before the grave a silent prayer,
When sight illumed my eyeballs; I beheld
The light of God, my grandson, and the tomb."
That is the tale, sire, which the old man told.
    (*General confusion. In the course of this speech* BORIS
        *several times wipes his face with his handkerchief.*)
To Uglich then I went, where it was learned
That many sufferers had likewise found
Deliverance at the grave of the Czarevitch.
This is my counsel; to the Kremlin send
The sacred relics, place them in the Minster
Of the Archangel; clearly will the people
See then the godless villain's fraud; the fiends'
Dread might will vanish as a cloud of dust.
                                    (*Silence.*)

SHUISKY. What mortal, holy father, knoweth the ways
Of the All-Highest? 'Tis not for me to judge him.
Untainted sleep and power of wonder-working
He may upon the child's remains bestow;
But vulgar rumor must dispassionately
And diligently be tested; is it for us,
In stormy times of insurrection,
To weigh so great a matter? Will men not say
That insolently we made of sacred things
A worldly instrument? Even now the people
Sway madly first this way, then that, even now
There are enough already of loud rumors;
This is no time to vex the people's minds
With aught so unexpectedly, grave, and strange.
I myself see 'tis needful to demolish

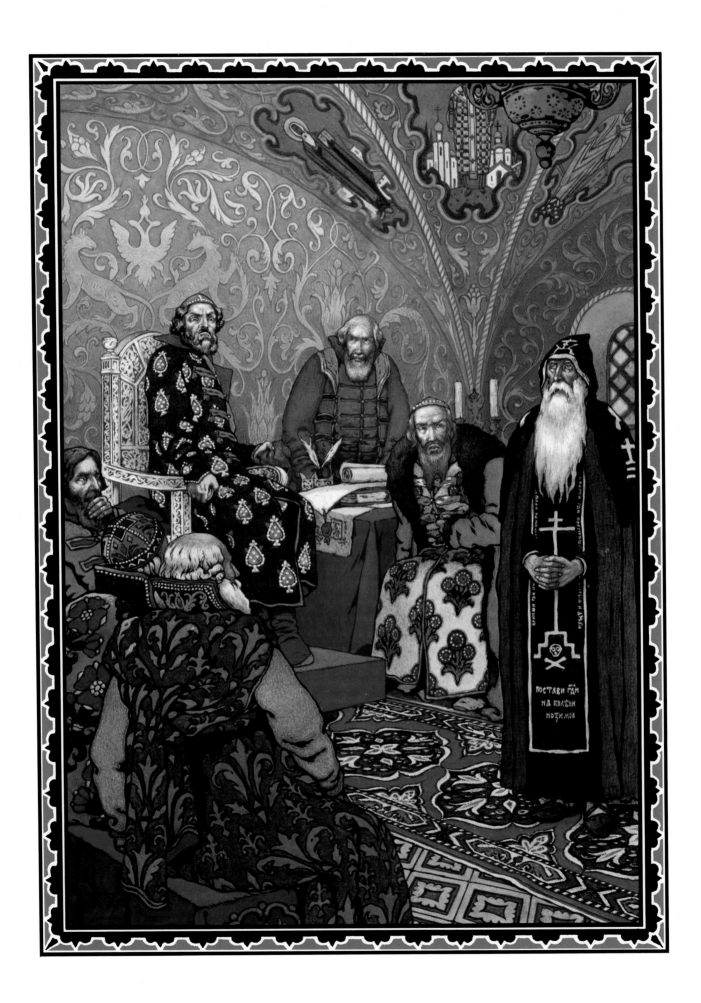

The rumor broadcast by the unfrocked monk;
But for this end other and simpler means
Will serve. Therefore, when it shall please thee, sire,
I will myself appear in public places,
I will dispel and exorcise this madness,
And will expose the vagabond's vile fraud.

CZAR. So be it! My lord Patriarch, I pray thee
Go with us to the palace, where today
I must converse with thee.
                    (*Exeunt; all the* BOYARS *follow them.*)

FIRST BOYAR. (*Sotto voce to another.*) Didst mark how
Pale our sovereign turned, how from his face there
Poured a mighty sweat?

SECOND BOYAR.        I durst not, I confess,
Uplift mine eyes, nor breathe, nor even stir.

FIRST BOYAR. Prince Shuisky's saved the day. A
Splendid fellow!


# A PLAIN NEAR NOVGOROD-SEVERSK


(*21 December 1604*)


SOLDIERS. (*Run in disorder.*) Woe, woe! The Czarevitch!
The Poles! There they are! There they are!
        (*Enter* CAPTAINS MARGERET *and* WALTER ROSEN.)

MARGERET. Whither, whither? Allons! Go back!

ONE OF THE FUGITIVES. You go back, if you like,
Cursed infidel.

MARGERET. Quoi, quoi?

ANOTHER. Quack! quack! You foreign frog, you like to
Croak at the Russian Czarevitch; but we—we are
Orthodox folk.

MARGERET. Qu'est-ce à dire "orthodox"? Sacrés gueux,
Maudite canaille! Mordieu, mein Herr, j'enrage; on
Dirait que sa n'a pas de bras pour frapper, sa n'a
Que des jambes pour foutre le camp.

ROSEN. Es ist Schande.

MARGERET. Ventre-saint gris! Je ne bouge plus d'un pas;
Puisque le vin est tiré, il faut le boire. Qu'en dites-
Vous, mein Herr?

ROSEN. Sie haben recht.

MARGERET. Tudieu, il y fait chaud! Ce diable de
"Pretender," comme ils l'appellent, est un bougre,
Qui a du poil au cul. Qu'en pensez-vous, mein Herr?

ROSEN. Oh, jà.

MARGERET. Hé! voyez donc, voyez donc! L'action
S'engage sur les derrières de l'ennemi. Ce doit être
Le brave Basmanov, qui aurait fait une sortie.

ROSEN. Ich glaube das.
                                         (*Enter* GERMANS.)

MARGERET. Ha, ha! voici nos allemands. Messieurs!
Mein Herr, dites-leur donc de se raillier et,
Sacrebleu, chargeons!

ROSEN. Sehr gut. Halt! (*The* GERMANS *fall into line.*)
Marsch!

THE GERMANS. (*They march.*) Hilf Gott!
> (*Fight. The* RUSSIANS *flee again.*)

POLES. Victory! Victory! Glory to the Czar Dimitry!

PRETENDER. (*On horseback.*) Cease firing. We have
Conquered. Enough! Spare Russian blood. Cease
Firing.
> (*Trumpets and drums.*)

# SQUARE IN FRONT OF THE CATHEDRAL IN MOSCOW

### THE PEOPLE

ONE MAN. Will the Czar soon come out of the
Cathedral?

ANOTHER. The mass is ended; now the Te Deum is
Going on.

FIRST MAN. What! Have they already cursed *him?*

SECOND MAN. I stood on the porch and heard how the
Deacon cried out: Grishka Otrepyev is anathema!

FIRST MAN. Let them curse to their heart's content; the
Czarevitch has nothing to do with Otrepyev.

SECOND MAN. But they are now singing mass for the
Repose of the soul of the Czarevitch.

FIRST MAN. What? A mass for the dead sung for a
Living man? They'll suffer for it, the godless wretches!

THIRD MAN. Hist! A noise. Is it not the Czar?

FOURTH MAN. No, it is the idiot.
    (*A saintly* IDIOT *enters, in an iron cap, hung round
      with chains; he is surrounded by* BOYS.)

BOYS. Nick, Nick, iron nightcap! T-r-r-r-r—

OLD WOMAN. Let the saintly one alone, you young devils.
    Pray for me, Nick, sinner that I am.

IDIOT. Give, give, give a penny.

OLD WOMAN. There is a penny for thee; remember me
    In thy prayers.

IDIOT. (*Seats himself on the ground and sings.*)

> The moon sails on,
> The kitten cries,
> Nick, arise,
> Pray to God.
>     (*The* BOYS *surround him again.*)

BOY. How do you do, Nick? Why don't you take off
    Your cap?
                    (*Raps him on the iron cap.*)
    How it rings!

IDIOT. But I have got a penny.

BOY. That's not true; now, show it.
             (*He snatches the penny and runs away.*)

IDIOT. (*Weeps.*) They have taken my penny, they
    Are hurting Nick!

THE PEOPLE. The Czar, the Czar is coming!
    (*The* CZAR *comes out from the cathedral; a* BOYAR
      in front of him scatters alms among the beggars.*)

IDIOT. Boris, Boris! The boys are hurting Nick.

CZAR. Give him alms! What is he crying about?

IDIOT. Little children are hurting Nick. . . . Have them Killed, as thou hadst the little Czarevitch killed.

BOYARS. Go away, fool! Seize the fool!

CZAR. Leave him alone. Pray thou for me, poor Nick.
(*Exit.*)

IDIOT. (*Calling after him.*) No, no! It is impossible to Pray for Czar Herod; the Mother of God forbids it.


# SEVSK

*The* PRETENDER, *surrounded by his supporters*

PRETENDER. Where is the prisoner?

A POLE.                                   Here.

PRETENDER.                    Call him before me.
(*Enter a* RUSSIAN *prisoner.*)
Who art thou? Speak.

PRISONER.          Rozhnov, a nobleman of Moscow.

PRETENDER. Hast long been in the service?

PRISONER.                              Nigh a month.

PRETENDER. Art not ashamed, Rozhnov, that thou hast drawn the sword against me?

PRISONER.            What else could I do?
  'Twas not our wish.

PRETENDER.         Didst fight beneath the walls
  Of Seversk?

PRISONER.    'Twas two weeks after the battle
  I came from Moscow.

PRETENDER.           What of Godounov?

PRISONER. The battle's loss, Mstislavsky's wound, hath
  Caused him much apprehension; Shuisky he hath
  Sent to take command.

PRETENDER.         But why hath he recalled
  Basmanov unto Moscow?

PRISONER.          The Czar rewarded
  His services with honor and with gold.
  Basmanov now sits in the council of
  The Czar.

PRETENDER. The army had more need of him.
  Well, how go things in Moscow?

PRISONER.            All is quiet,
  Thank God.

PRETENDER.  Say, do they look for me?

PRISONER.             God knows;
  They dare not talk too much there now. For some
  Have had their tongues cut off, and others even
  Their heads. It is a fearsome state of things—
  Each day an execution. All the prisons
  Are crammed. Wherever two or three foregather
  In public places, instantly a spy
  Worms himself in; the Czar himself examines

At leisure the informers. It is just
Sheer misery; so silence is the best.

PRETENDER. An enviable life for that Czar's people!
Well, and what of the army?

PRISONER.                          What of it?
Clothed and full-fed, the army is content.

PRETENDER. But is it very large?

PRISONER.                          God knows.

PRETENDER.                                   All told
Will there be thirty thousand?

PRISONER.                          Yes; 'twill run
Even to fifty thousand.
     (*The* PRETENDER *reflects; those around him glance*
          *at one another.*)

PRETENDER.               Well! What say
They in your camp of me?

PRISONER.                    Why, of thy grace
They say, sire (be not wroth), that thou'rt a knave,
And yet, forsooth, a man of pluck.

PRETENDER. (*Laughing.*)               Even so
I'll prove myself to them in deed. My friends,
We will not wait for Shuisky; give you joy;
Tomorrow, battle.
                                        (*Exit.*)


ALL.                    Long life to Dimitry!

A POLE. Tomorrow, battle! They are fifty thousand,
And we scarce fifteen thousand. He is mad!

ANOTHER. That's nothing, friend. A single Pole can
  Challenge five hundred Muscovites.

PRISONER.                    Yes, thou mayst challenge!
  But when it comes to fighting, then, thou braggart,
  Thou'lt run away.

POLE.             If thou hadst had a sword,
  Insolent prisoner, then (*pointing to his sword*) with
  This I'd soon have mastered thee.

PRISONER.             A Russian can make shift
  Without a sword; how like you this (*shows his fist*),
  You fool?
    (*The* POLE *looks at him haughtily and departs
      in silence. All laugh.*)


# A FOREST

(*In the background lies a dying horse*)

PRETENDER *and* PUSHKIN


PRETENDER. Ah, my poor horse! How gallantly
  He charged today in the last battle, and when
  Wounded, how swiftly bore me. My poor horse!

PUSHKIN. (*To himself.*)                    Well, here's
  A great ado about a horse, when all
  Our army's smashed to bits.

PRETENDER.                    Listen! Perhaps
   He's but exhausted by the loss of blood,
   And will recover.

PUSHKIN.              Nay, nay; he is dying.

PRETENDER. (*Goes to his horse.*)
   My poor horse! What to do? Take off the bridle,
   And loose the girth. Let him at least die free.
      (*He unbridles and unsaddles the horse. Some*
         POLES *enter.*)
   Good evening, gentlemen! How is't I see not
   Kurbsky among you? I did note today
   How he cut through to where the fight was thickest;
   Around the man, like swaying ears of corn,
   The sabers flashed; but higher than the rest
   His blade was brandished, and his mighty cry
   Drowned all cries else. Where is my knight?

POLE.                                    He fell
   Upon the field of battle.

PRETENDER.              Honor the brave,
   And peace be to his soul! How few unscathed
   Are left us from the fight! Accursed Cossacks,
   Traitors and miscreants, you, you it is
   Have ruined us! Not even for three minutes
   To keep the foe at bay! I'll teach the villains!
   Every tenth man I'll hang. Brigands!

PUSHKIN.                          Whoe'er
   Be guilty, all the same we were clean worsted,
   Routed!

PRETENDER. But yet we nearly conquered. Just
   When I had dealt with their front rank, the

Germans repulsed us utterly. But they're fine
Fellows! By God! Fine fellows! I do love them for it.
I'll form of them an honorable troop.

PUSHKIN. Where shall we spend the night?

PRETENDER.                                    Here, in the forest.
   Why not rest here tonight? And just at daybreak
   We'll take the road, and dine in Rylsk. Good night.
     (*He lies down, puts a saddle under his head, and*
       *falls asleep.*)

PUSHKIN. A pleasant sleep, Czarevitch! Smashed to
   Bits, rescued by flight alone, he is as careless
   As a mere child alone; 'tis clear that Providence
   Protects him, and we, friends, must not lose heart.

 LE PALAIS DU TSAR

## PALACE OF THE CZAR

(*Moscow, 1605*)

BORIS *and* BASMANOV

CZAR. He's vanquished, but what profit lies in that?
We are crowned with a vain conquest; he has
Mustered again his scattered forces, and anew
Threatens us from the ramparts of Putivl.
Meanwhile what are our heroes doing? They're
At Krom, where from its rotten battlements
A band of Cossacks braves them. There is glory!

99

No, I am ill content with them; thyself
I shall dispatch to take command of them;
I grant command not unto birth, but brains.
Their pride of precedence, let it be wounded!
The time has come for me to hold in scorn
The murmur of a worthless well-born mob,
And quash the vicious custom.

BASMANOV.                             Ay, my lord
Blessèd a hundredfold will be that day
When fire consumes the lists of noblemen
With their dissensions, their proud pedigrees.

CZAR. That day is not far off; let me but first
Subdue the insurrection of the people.

BASMANOV. Why trouble about that? The people
Always are ready for rebellion; even so
The swift steed champs the bit; so doth a lad
Chafe at his father's ruling. But what of it?
The rider quietly controls the steed,
The father sways the son.

CZAR.                             Sometimes the horse
Doth throw the rider, nor does the son at all times
Abide the father's will; we can restrain
The people only by unsleeping sternness.
So thought Ivan, sagacious autocrat
And storm-subduer; so his fierce grandson thought.
No, no, kindness is lost upon the people;
Do good—it thanks you not at all; extort
And execute—'twill be no worse for you.
                                        (*Enter a* BOYAR.)
What now?

BOYAR.        The foreign merchants, sire.

CZAR.                                              I go
To welcome them. Basmanov, wait, stay here;

I still have need to speak a word with thee.
                                        (*Exit.*)

BASMANOV. High sovereign spirit! God grant he may
    Subdue the accurst Otrepyev; and much, still much
    Of good he'll do for Russia. A great thought
    Within his mind has taken birth; it must not
    Be suffered to grow cold. What a career
    For me when once he crushes the proud might
    Of the nobility. I have no rivals
    In war. I shall stand closest to the throne—
    And it may chance— But what is that strange noise?
        (*Alarm.* BOYARS *and* COURT-ATTENDANTS *run in
            disorder, meet and whisper.*)

ONE ATTENDANT. Fetch a physician!

ANOTHER.                          Quickly to the Patriarch!

A THIRD. He calls for the Czarevitch, the Czarevitch!

A FOURTH. Call a priest!

BASMANOV.               What has happened?

A FIFTH AND SIXTH.                          The Czar's ill.
    The Czar is dying.

BASMANOV.          Good God!

A FIFTH.                          On the throne
    He sat, and suddenly he fell; blood gushed
    From mouth and ears.
        (*The* CZAR *is carried in on a chair. All the Czar's
            household; all the* BOYARS.)

CZAR.          Let all depart—alone
    Leave the Czarevitch with me. (*All withdraw.*)

I am dying; let us embrace. Farewell, my son;
Forthwith thou wilt begin to reign. O God, my God!
Forthwith, I shall appear before thy presence—
And now I have not time to shrive my soul.
But yet, my son, I feel thou'rt dearer to me
Than is my soul's salvation—be it so!
A subject was I born; it seemed ordained
That I should die a subject in obscurity.
Yet I attained to sovereignty; but how?
Ask not. Enough that thou art innocent.
Thou wilt reign rightfully; and I alone
Am answerable for all to God. Dear son,
Cherish no false delusion, of thy free will
Blind not thyself. Stormy the days wherein
Thou dost assume the crown. He is dangerous,
This strange pretender; with a fearful name
He is weaponed. I at last with years grown skilled
In ruling could full well put down rebellion;
They quaked with fear before me; treachery
Dared not to raise its voice; but thou, a boy,
An inexperienced ruler, how wilt thou
Govern amid the tempests, quench revolt,
Shackle sedition? But God is great! He gives
Wisdom to youth, to weakness strength. Give ear:
Firstly, select a steadfast counselor,
Cool, of ripe years, loved of the people, honored
Mid the boyars for birth and fame—say, Shuisky.
The army craves today a skillful leader;
Appoint Basmanov; do not heed the murmurs
Of the boyars. Thou from thy early years
Didst sit with me in council, thou dost know
The formal course of government; change not
Procedure. Custom is the soul of states.
Of late I have been driven to restore
Bans, executions—these thou canst rescind;
And they will bless thee, as they blessed thy uncle
When he succeeded to the Terrible.
At the same time, little by little, tighten
Anew the reins of government; now slacken;

But let them not slip from thy hands. Be gracious,
Accessible to foreigners, accept
Their service trustfully. Preserve with strictness
The Church's discipline. Be taciturn;
The royal voice must never lose itself
Upon the air in vain; it must be like
A sacred bell that sounds but to announce
Some great disaster or great festival.
Dear son, thou art approaching to those years
When woman's beauty agitates our blood.
Preserve, preserve the sacred purity
Of innocence and haughty modesty;
He, who through passion has been wont to wallow
In vicious pleasures in his youthful days,
Becomes in manhood bloodthirsty and surly;
His mind untimely darkens. Of thy household
Be always head; show honor to thy mother,
But rule thy house thyself; thou art a man
And czar to boot. Be tender to thy sister—
For thou art now, alas, her sole protector.

FEODOR. (*On his knees.*) No, no; live on, my father,
   And reign long; without thee both the folk and
   We will perish.

CZAR. For me all's at an end—mine eyes grow dark,
   I feel the coldness of the grave—
       (*Enter the* PATRIARCH *and* PRELATES, *followed by
         all the* BOYARS. *The* CZARINA *is supported on
         either side; the* CZAREVNA *is sobbing.*)
                   Who's there?
   Ah, 'tis the vestment—so! the holy vows—
   The hour has struck. The Czar becomes a monk,
   And the dark sepulchre will be my cell.
   Wait yet a little, my lord Patriarch,
   I still am Czar. Listen to me, boyars:
   To this my son I now commit the czardom;
   Do homage to Feodor. Basmanov, thou,
   And ye, my friends, on the grave's brink I pray you

To serve my son with zeal and rectitude!
As yet he is both young and uncorrupted.
Swear ye?

BOYARS.      We swear.

CZAR.                    I am content. Forgive me
My sins and my surrenders to temptation,
The harm I meant and that I did not mean.
Approach now, holy father; I am ready.
   (*The rite begins. The women, who have swooned,
   are carried out.*)


# ARMY HEADQUARTERS

BASMANOV *leads in* PUSHKIN


BASMANOV. Here enter, and speak freely. So to me
   He sent thee.

PUSHKIN.        He doth offer thee his friendship
   And the next place to his in Muscovy.

BASMANOV. But even thus highly by Feodor am I
   Already raised; the army I command;
   For me he scorned nobility of rank
   And the wrath of the boyars. I swore allegiance
   To him.

PUSHKIN.  Thou'st sworn allegiance to the man
   Who lawfully succeedeth to the throne;
   Suppose that there is one whose rights are greater.

BASMANOV. Enough; tell me no idle tales! I know
   Who the man is.

PUSHKIN.                    Russia and Lithuania
    Have long acknowledged him to be Dimitry;
    But, be that as it may, I don't insist.
    Perchance he is indeed the real Dimitry;
    Perchance but a pretender; only this
    I know, that soon or late Boris's son
    Will yield Moscow to him.

BASMANOV.                        So long as I
    Stand by the youthful Czar, so long he will not
    Forsake the throne. We have sufficient troops,
    Thank God! With victory I will inspire them.
    And whom do you intend to send against me:
    Is it Karela, is it Mniszech? Are
    Your numbers many? You have scarce
    Eight thousand.

PUSHKIN. Indeed thou art mistaken: they will not
    Amount even to that. I say myself
    Our army is mere trash, the Cossacks only
    Rob villages, the Poles but brag and drink;
    The Russians—what shall I say?—with thee I'll not
    Dissemble; but, Basmanov, dost thou know
    Wherein our true strength lies? Not in the army,
    Nor yet in Polish aid, but in opinion—
    Yes, popular opinion. Dost remember
    The triumph of Dimitry, dost remember
    His peaceful conquests, when, without a blow,
    The docile towns surrendered, and the mob
    Bound the recalcitrant leaders? Thou thyself
    Wast witness; was it willingly your troops
    Waged war against him? Aye, and when? Boris
    Was then supreme. But would they now? Nay, nay,
    It is too late to blow on the cold embers
    Of this dispute; with all thy wits and firmness
    Thou'lt not withstand him. Were it not far better
    If thou wouldst be the one to take the lead,
    Proclaim Dimitry Czar, and by that act
    Bind him thy friend forever? How thinkest thou?

BASMANOV. Tomorrow thou shalt know.

PUSHKIN.                                    Resolve.

BASMANOV.                                    Farewell.

PUSHKIN. Ponder it well, Basmanov.

                                    (*Exit.*)

BASMANOV.                         He is right.
   Everywhere treason ripens; what's to do?
   Wait, that the rebels may deliver me
   In bonds to this Otrepyev? Had I not better
   Forestall the stormy onset of the flood,
   Myself to—ah! but to forswear mine oath!
   Incurring fresh disgrace from age to age!
   The trust of my young sovereign to requite
   With horrible betrayal! 'Tis a light thing
   For a dishonored exile to be plotting
   Sedition and conspiracy; but I?
   Is it for me, the favorite of my lord?
   But death—but power—the people's miseries . . .
                                    (*He ponders.*)
   Who's there? (*Whistles.*) A horse here!
   Sound the muster-drum!

# PLACE OF EXECUTION
# RED SQUARE, MOSCOW

PUSHKIN *enters, surrounded by the* PEOPLE

THE PEOPLE. Here cometh a boyar from the Czarevitch.
   Let's hear what the boyar will tell us. Hither!
   Hither!

PUSHKIN. (*On a platform.*) Townsmen of Moscow!
   The Czarevitch
   Bids me convey his greetings to you. (*He bows.*) Ye
   Know how Divine Providence saved the Czarevitch
   From the base murderer's hands; he marched to
   Punish his would-be murderer, but God already
   Had struck him down. All Russia hath submitted
   Unto Dimitry; with sincere repentance
   Basmanov hath himself led forth his troops
   To swear allegiance to him. With love and peace
   Dimitry comes to you. Would ye, to please
   The house of Godounov, uplift a hand
   Against the lawful Czar, against the grandson
   Of Monomakh?

THE PEOPLE.       Not we.

PUSHKIN.            Townsmen of Moscow!
   The world well knows how much ye have endured
   The while the harsh usurper ruled you; ban,
   Dishonor, executions, taxes, hardships,
   Hunger—all these ye have experienced.
   Dimitry is disposed to show you favor,
   Courtiers, boyars, soldiers, and functionaries,
   Merchants—and all the honest folk. And will ye
   Be stubborn without reason, and in pride
   Flee from his kindness? But he himself is coming
   To his ancestral throne with mighty escort.
   Provoke not ye the Czar to wrath, fear God,
   And swear allegiance to the lawful ruler;
   Humble yourselves; forthwith send to Dimitry
   The Metropolitan, boyars, officials,
   And chosen men, that they may all do homage
   To him who is their lord and father.
                 (*Exit. Clamor of the* PEOPLE.)

THE PEOPLE.                    Well?
   He spoke the truth. Long live our lord, Dimitry!

A PEASANT ON THE PLATFORM. Folk! To the Kremlin!
    To the royal palace!
To bind Boris's whelp!

THE PEOPLE. (*Rushing in a crowd.*)
                    Bind, drown him! Hail
Dimitry! Crush the race of Godounov!


# THE KREMLIN.
# HOUSE OF BORIS

A GUARD *on the steps*, FEODOR *at a*
*window*, BEGGAR, THE PEOPLE


BEGGAR. Alms, for Christ's sake!

GUARD. Go away; it is forbidden to speak to the
    Prisoners.

FEODOR. Go, old man, I am poorer than thou; thou art
    At liberty.
            (XENIA, *veiled, also comes to the window.*)

ONE OF THE PEOPLE. Brother and sister—poor children,
    Like birds in a cage.

ANOTHER. So you've pity for them? Accursèd house!

FIRST MAN. The father was a villain, but the children
    Are innocent.

SECOND MAN. The apple does not fall far from the
    Apple-tree.

XENIA. Dear brother! dear brother! I think the boyars
    Are coming to us.

FEODOR. That is Golitsyn, Mosalsky. I do not know the
Others.

XENIA. Ah! dear brother, my heart sinks.
    (GOLITSYN, MOSALSKY, MOLCHANOV, *and*
      SHEREFEDINOV; *behind them three* SOLDIERS.)

THE PEOPLE. Make way, make way; the boyars are
    coming.                   (*They enter the house.*)

ONE OF THE PEOPLE. What have they come for?

ANOTHER. Most like to make Feodor Godounov swear
    Allegiance.

A THIRD. Very like. Hark! what a noise in the house!
    What an uproar! They are fighting!

THE PEOPLE. Do you hear? A scream! That was a
    Woman's voice. Let us go up! The doors are locked—
    The cries have ceased.
      (*The doors are thrown open.* MOSALSKY *appears*
        *on the steps.*)

MOSALSKY. Good folk! Maria Godounov and her son
    Feodor have poisoned themselves. We have seen
    Their dead bodies.
          (*The* PEOPLE *are silent with horror.*)
    Why are ye silent? Cry, Long live Czar Dimitry
    Ivanovich!
          (*The* PEOPLE *are speechless.*)